••• Pauline Cullen

Common mistakes at

IELTS Intermediate

... and how to avoid them

CAMBRIDGE
UNIVERSITY PRESS

CAMBRIDGE UNIVERSITY PRESS
Cambridge, New York, Melbourne, Madrid, Cape Town, Singapore,
São Paulo, Delhi, Dubai, Tokyo

Cambridge University Press
The Edinburgh Building, Cambridge CB2 8RU, UK

www.cambridge.org
Information on this title: www.cambridge.org/9780521692465

First published 2007
4th printing 2010

Printed in Dubai by Oriental Press

A catalogue record for this publication is available from the British Library

ISBN 978-0-521-69246-5 Paperback

Produced by Kamae Design

Contents

Are there any special times I should use *the*?

1 **Tick the correct sentence in each pair.**

1 a In the USA this situation is totally different.
  b In USA this situation is totally different.
2 a The table shows number of people working in Britain in 1976.
  b The table shows the number of people working in Britain in 1976.

We use *the*
- with countries or places where the name refers to a group of islands or states: *the United States, the Middle East, the United Arab Emirates, the UK*
- with superlatives: *the best, the longest, the highest*
- with cardinal numbers: *the first, the second, the third*
- when there is only one in the world: *the environment, the internet, the sun*
- to refer to the only one in this particular area: *the government, the police, the river*
- in the phrase: *the same as*

We don't use *the*
- with a single country or place: *America, England, China*
- to talk about something in general. We use the plural if we are talking about something in general; we use *the* to identify one specific example. Compare:
  *People with reading difficulties often have problems with **numbers**.*
  ***The number** eight is considered lucky in some countries.*

2 Correct the mistake below.

Your hairstyle is not same as mine.

Your hairstyle is ....

3 **Complete the sentences below using the words in brackets. Decide whether or not to use *the*, or whether to use the plural.**

1 The main advantage of .... is that it gives us access to information from all over the world. (*internet*)
2 My father has fished in .... all over Australia. (*river*)
3 Life in .... is very different from life in my country. (*America*)
4 According to the graph, ... of people moving into the city each year has more than doubled. (*number*)
5 The total figure for 1976 was .... as the total figure for 1982. (*same*)
6 Obesity is much more common in .... than in my country. (*USA*)
7 The graph shows that .... increase occurred in 1999. (*greatest*)
8 .... travels around .... at a speed of 3,700 kilometres per hour. (*moon, earth*)

2 Singular or plural?

1 Tick the correct sentence in each pair.

1 a There are several problem with this idea.
  b There are several problems with this idea.
2 a Many charity organisations provide a great deal of help.
  b Many charity organisation provides a great deal of help.

If you use a plural noun, you must use a plural verb. The verb must 'agree' with the noun:

*In my country **there are** very few **cars** that use leaded petrol.* (plural verb + plural noun)
*I like studying during the day but **my friend prefers** studying at night.* (singular noun + singular verb)

We use a plural noun with:
- plural verbs: *are, were, have, do, play*, etc.: ***There are** a lot of **books** on the table.*
- numbers greater than one: *30 **cars**, 100 **students***
- *many*: *It is annoying that so **many buses drive** past because they **are** full.*
- *the number of*: ***The number of buses** on our roads **has** increased each year.*

☆ Note that we use a plural noun but a singular verb after *the number of*.

We use a singular noun with:
- singular verbs: *is, was, has, does, plays*, etc.: ***There is** only one **bedroom** in the flat.*
- *a/an* or *one*: *a car, one student*

☆ Note that some nouns can look plural but are singular (*news, mathematics*) and some nouns have a different form in the plural (*children, men, women, people*).

2 Correct the mistake below.

The number of woman studying science increased dramatically last year.

The number of .... dramatically last year.

3 Underline the correct word in each sentence.

1 The *childs / children* are playing in the street.
2 The number of *men / man* studying science has decreased.
3 There are a lot of *persons / people* in my class.
4 I enjoyed studying mathematics a lot; I found *it / them* very interesting.
5 The news *were / was* very upsetting.
6 How many *classes / class* do you have today?
7 A *person / people* I really admire is my uncle.
8 My father *watch / watches* a lot of sport on TV.

Which nouns don't have a plural form?

1 Tick the correct sentence in each pair.

1 a I don't have many time to complete my assignment.
   b I don't have much time to complete my assignment.

2 a When I did a search on my computer, I could only find a few informations about the topic.
   b When I did a search on my computer, I could only find a little information about the topic.

Some nouns in English are 'uncountable'. This means they do not have a plural form. Some common uncountable nouns are: *advice, advertising, food, furniture, garbage, information, knowledge, money, shopping, time, traffic, travel.*

With uncountable nouns, you must use:
* the singular form: *food, information, money*
* *a little / amount of / much / some*: *How **much money** do you have?*
  *The **amount of traffic** on the roads is increasing each year.*
* a singular verb: *There **was** already a little **furniture** in the flat.*

If a noun is uncountable, you cannot use:
* a plural form: ~~advices, furnitures, garbages, informations, knowledges~~
* *a/an*: ~~an advice, a garbage, a knowledge~~
* *a few / many / number of*: ~~a few shopping, many traffic, the number of knowledge~~
* a number: ~~three travels, four furniture~~
* a plural verb: ~~There were a little furniture in the flat.~~
☆ If you want to add a number to an uncountable noun, you can use *a piece of / some / a few pieces of*: *a piece of advice, three pieces of furniture, a few pieces of garbage*

2 Correct the mistake below.

> The number of garbages we produce is increasing.

The .... we produce is increasing.

3 Correct the mistakes in these sentences. There may be more than one mistake in each sentence.

1 My tutor was very helpful; he gave me one very good advice about how to study.
2 I was surprised by the number of times it took us to reach the castle.
3 You need a great deal of knowledges to become a doctor.
4 The informations we were given by the tour guide were not very helpful.
5 When we visited the park, we were upset to see so many garbages left there.
6 We arrived late because there were so many traffic on the road.
7 I can't wait to visit the market and do a few shopping.
8 The furnitures in the hotel room were quite old but they were very comfortable.

1 Underline the correct word or phrase in the following sentences.

1 The garbage *is* / *are* collected every Tuesday.
2 Advertising in the school newsletter *is* / *are* a waste of time.
3 A lot of food in restaurants *is* / *are* thrown away every day.
4 Many *idea* / *ideas* for new products never reach the manufacturing stage.
5 My sister gave me lots of *advice* / *advices* that *was* / *were* very useful.
6 Over three hundred *student* / *students* signed the petition for a new study area.
7 There are a lot of *similarity* / *similarities* between your country and mine.
8 There *is* / *are* more women on my course than men.

2 Fill in the gaps using one of the words from the box. Decide whether you need to add *the*.

Rank	Country	Number of people accessing the internet per 100,000 people
#1	New Zealand	79.306
#2	Iceland	76.027
#3	Sweden	75.539
#4	Malta	75.527
#5	Faroe Islands	68.140
#6	Greenland	67.406
#7	Korea, South	64.925
#8	Australia	64.709
#9	Finland	62.914
#10	United Kingdom	62.209

Faroe Islands	**internet**	**largest**	**list**	**Malta**	**number one**
same	**Sweden**	**table**	**United Kingdom**	**United States**	**world**

(1)........................ shows the top ten countries in terms of internet usage.
(2)........................ country is New Zealand, which has (3)........................ number of
internet users. (4)........................ is at the bottom of (5)........................ . Surprisingly,
(6)........................ does not feature in the top ten at all. However, a little-known group
of islands called (7)........................ is ranked fifth in (8)........................ . (9)........................
and (10)........................ are ranked third and fourth. Both have almost
(11)........................ number of users, with over 75,500 people per 100,000 accessing
(12)........................ .

3 Look at the following advertisement and fill in the gap in each question using one of the phrases in the box.

How many	How much	Is	Are	Is there	Are there

Room for rent in share house close to bus. Must help to pay bills (electricity, etc.). For more details phone: 376 8900

1 .... food included in the rent?
2 .... a lot of traffic in the area?
3 .... any other transport nearby?
4 .... does the electricity usually cost?
5 .... any pets in the house?
6 .... money will I need to pay each week?
7 .... people are living in the house?
8 .... a lot of furniture in the room?

4 Fill in the blanks using a word from the box. Make any changes necessary.

advice	bird	child	company	house	person	plastic	transport

1 The travel agency was hopeless; they didn't even give us one useful ....
2 The number of new .... being built in our area has doubled.
3 Most large .... operate on a global scale nowadays.
4 Many .... believe that globalisation has both advantages and disadvantages.
5 Today, in my country, school-age .... do not exercise as much as in the past.
6 The blades of the fan are made of ....
7 There are several kinds of .... in my home town but my favourite is the ferry.
8 There has been an increase in the number of native .... killed by cats this year.

5 Correct the 14 mistakes in the text below.

The globalisation has had an enormous impact on many part of the world. Nowadays, even in some of most remote parts of world, we can connect to internet and conduct business. However, they is advantage and disadvantage to this. One disadvantages, for example, is that the local culture and language can be affected. It can also mean that local businesses has to reduce their prices to compete with bigger overseas companies. However, there are advantages; for example, globalisation can bring more business to a small area, which is good for the local economy. It may also help to stop young person moving away from more remote area. If a young person have the chance to run a business and be successful no matter where he or she lives, then perhaps more people will choose to stay in these smaller communities. It also means that news from around the world are available to everyone, and this can also reduce the feeling of isolation.

When do I use the present simple tense?

1 Choose the correct sentence in each pair.

1 a Nowadays, our bodies becoming 'old' much later than 100 years ago.

   b Nowadays, our bodies become 'old' much later than 100 years ago.

2 a Children lost their freedom if they have too many responsibilities.

   b Children lose their freedom if they have too many responsibilities.

We use the present simple tense:

- to make general statements about our world: *The earth **moves** around the sun.*
- to show a pattern or general truth: *People **work** in order to meet their basic needs.*
- with adverbs of frequency: *always, usually, often, sometimes, never. People who are too lazy to walk **often use** their cars instead.*
- with expressions such as: *nowadays, these days, today* (with a general meaning): *Many students **today do** their research via computer rather than through books.*
- for verbs showing opinions or feelings, e.g. *believe, think, hope*: *I **think** that we should all do as much as we can to improve our environment.*

We form the present simple tense with the base form of the verb. We add *s* or *es* to form the 3rd person singular:

I play	*I watch*
you play	*you watch*
he/she/it plays	*he/she/it watches*
we play	*we watch*
you play	*you watch*
they play	*they watch*

2 Correct the mistake below.

My brother watch TV for 8 hours every day.

My brother ....

3 Correct the mistakes in the sentences below.

1 People should act according to what they are believing.

2 In general, I think our government spent too much money on space travel.

3 Nowadays, many people in my country have sent their children to single-sex schools.

4 These days, more and more people travelling to very distant places for their holidays.

5 I am hoping it is not too late to save the environment.

6 The female hen laying on average 5 or 6 eggs per week.

7 Younger drivers is more likely to be involved in a car accident.

8 Most doctors are agreeing that the only way to lose weight is by doing more exercise.

How do I write large numbers?

1 Tick the correct sentence in each pair.

1 a The government spent ten millions dollars on education last year.
   b The government spent ten million dollars on education last year.
2 a There were thousands of people at the football match.
   b There were a thousand of people at the football match.

When we talk about a specific large number, we do not add *s* to the number:
200,000 = *two hundred **thousand*** (not ~~two hundred thousands~~)
10,000,000 = *ten **million*** (not ~~ten millions~~)
The noun that follows is always plural:
*There must have been at least three thousand **students** at the protest.*
We use the plural form of large numbers + *of* to give an approximate idea of how many:
*There must have been **thousands of** students at the protest.*

We can use *a* instead of *one*. *One* is more formal:
*If I won **a million** dollars, I would probably take a year off and travel around the world.*
*The president promised to increase the health budget by **one million** dollars.*

☆ We usually use numerals for numbers that cannot be written in one or two words:
*More than **two million** people attended last year.* but: *2,001,967 people attended last year.*

You should write fractions in words: *half a (million); a/one third of a (million); three quarters of a (million); one and a quarter (million); one and three quarter (million)*:
*According to the chart, in 2004 over **half a million** Ukranians went to the cinema.*

2 Correct the mistake below.

A thousands of people came to see the royal wedding.

.... came to see the royal wedding.

3 Underline the correct number in the sentences below.

1 The skeleton had remained hidden for *a thousands / thousands* of years.
2 The chart shows that *three hundreds / three hundred* whales were seen here in 1990.
3 *Three and a half billion / three and a half of a billion* will watch the ceremony .
4 I pay *six hundred dollars / six hundred dollar* rent each month.
5 Real estate in my city is very expensive; a small house can cost *three quarter of a million / three quarters of a million* dollars.
6 *A million of / Millions of* dollars are spent on space exploration each year.
7 By 2005, more than *six hundred / six hundreds of* children were enrolled in the school.
8 The company has sold *one and a half billions / one and a half billion* computers so far.

6 There is / there are

1 Tick the correct sentence in each pair.

1 a It is a lovely park near my house.
   b There is a lovely park near my house.
2 a There have very good restaurants and shops on board the ship.
   b There are very good restaurants and shops on board the ship.

We use *there* to say that something exists. We use *there is* with a singular subject and *there are* with a plural subject:
There is an oak **tree** in my garden. (not ~~It is an oak tree~~ or ~~There have an oak tree~~)
There are some great **movies** on at the cinema. (not ~~They are some great movies~~)

We use *there is* and *there are* to give new information. We use *it is* or *they are* to talk about something that has already been referred to. Compare:
There is a present for you on the table. (the first time the present has been mentioned)
Mary: *What is **that** you're carrying?*
John: ***It's** a present for my sister.* (it = what John is carrying)

We do not use the auxiliary verb *do* to form questions and negatives with *there is* and *there are*: **Are there** any clean glasses in the cupboard? **There isn't** a map in the car.
☆ *There* cannot be left out: **There is** a pan of soup and **there are** some bowls in the kitchen. (not ~~There is a pan of soup and are some bowls in the kitchen.~~)

2 Correct the mistake below.

> Before they built the supermarket, there had a lot more little shops in the high street.

Before they built the supermarket, ... in the high street.

3 Correct the mistakes in the sentences below.

1 In developed countries there is many possible solutions to this problem.
2 There no clear trend in the data shown in graph 1.
3 There is no electricity and are no factories in this area.
4 Fortunately, they are still a lot of good people in the world.
5 It is a very small village so there don't have any large supermarkets.
6 In the first chart, it is a large gap between the cost of living and salaries earned.
7 In 1990 there was 3 million people working in this industry.
8 How much work there is to do?

Test 2

1 Fill in the gaps with the correct form of the verbs in brackets.

Examiner: Can you describe a typical morning at your house?

Candidate: Well, my father always (1) .... (*get up*) first because he (2)........................ (*start*) work at 7 o'clock. The traffic (3) .... (*be*) very bad in my city so he (4) .... (*have*) to leave at 6 o'clock. Before he (5) .... (*leave*), he (6) .... (*wake*) my brother and me up. I (7) .... (*get up*) straight away but my brother (8) .... (*prefer*) to sleep as long as he can, and he nearly always (9) .... (*catch*) the last bus to school. My mother (10) .... (*make*) our breakfast while I (11) .... (*get dressed*), then I (12) .... (*leave*) for school at about 7.30.

2 Match each amount (1–5) with its correct written equivalent (a–i). You'll need to read the words carefully.

1	$305,000	a	thrity-five dollars
		b	three and a half million dollars
2	$35	c	three hundreds and five dollar
		d	thirty five thousands dollars
3	$35,000	e	three millions and five hundred thousands dollars
		f	thirty-five dollars
4	$3,500,000	g	three hundred and five thousand dollars
		h	thirty-five thousand dollars
5	$305	i	three hundred and five dollars

3 Find 12 mistakes in the essay below and correct them.

In my country agriculture are very important. Each year our farmers growing a wide variety of crops and this helped to reduce the amount of food we need to import, which also reduced the price of fresh food in the shops. Life is sometimes difficult for farmers because their day begun very early and they often works until late at night. The weather also is making their working conditions very difficult at times. What is more, many farmers are feeling that they do not receive a fair price for their products. We are need to encourage farmers to stay in this industry. Nowadays, big supermarket chains taking a large amount of the profits that should go to the farmers. The government needed to address this situation and make sure that they protecting this vital industry.

4 Fill in the blanks in the text with numbers from the table. Three of your answers should contain a fraction.

Number of tractors used in agriculture: top ten countries		
Rank	Country	Amount
#1	United States	4,800,000
#2	Japan	2,028,000
#3	Italy	1,750,000
#4	India	1,525,000
#5	Poland	1,306,700
#6	France	1,264,000
#7	Germany	1,030,800
#8	Turkey	905,000
#9	Spain	885,000
#10	China	755,073

SOURCE: World Resources Institute

The table shows the number of tractors being used by the top ten countries in the world. The United States has the greatest number of tractors, with almost (1)........*five million*........ . Japan has less than half of this amount, with just over (2).. , and Italy is ranked third, with a total of (3)...................................... . India has just over (4).. , while Poland, France and Germany each have over (5).. . Of the bottom three countries on this list, Turkey has a little under (6).. , Spain has less than (7).. and China has just over (8).. tractors.

5 Fill in the gaps in the following sentences with either *it*, *they* or *there*.

1 .... are several reasons why I wanted to talk to you.
2 I have printed out the letters. .... are on the desk ready for you to sign.
3 On the next street corner .... is an excellent new restaurant.
4 .... have a wonderful swimming pool in this hotel.
5 We had a lovely holiday in Florence. .... really is a beautiful city.
6 .... were several robberies in the area last week.
7 Were your parents born here or did .... move here from another country?
8 Is .... going to be a meeting this week?

Which relative pronoun should I use?

1 Tick the correct sentence in each pair.

1 a You should do that what you think is right.
 b You should do what you think is right.
2 a There are several factors that are important in achieving happiness.
 b There are several factors are important in achieving happiness.

Relative pronouns (*that, who*, etc.) are used to connect two separate clauses:

        clause 1   relative pronoun   clause 2
*There are several factors / **that** / are important in achieving happiness.*

When information is essential to the sentence and cannot be left out, we use:
* *that* to refer to things or people: *The **chart that** is on page 10 shows...*
* *who* to refer to people: *The number of **women who** were enrolled...*
* *what* to refer to *the thing that* or *the things that*: *The government should show us **what** must be done.* (= the thing(s) that must be done)

☆ Note that you should only use one relative pronoun (not ~~The government must show us that what needs to be done.~~).

The relative pronoun can be left out if it refers to the object of a verb, but not if it refers to the subject of a verb. Compare:
*The students **that** I teach all come from overseas countries. students* is the object of the verb *teach*, so the relative pronoun *that* can be left out: *The students I teach all come from...*
*The students **who** are studying EAP should see me today. students* is the subject of the verb *are studying*, so the relative pronoun *who* cannot be left out (not ~~The students are studying EAP should see me today.~~).

2 Correct the mistake below.

I need to find someone can play the piano for our assembly next month.

I need to find .... for our assembly next month.

3 Correct the mistakes in the sentences below.

1 This is one of the problems that what can occur when you spend too much money.
2 The teacher inspired me most at school was called Miss Gillies.
3 There are many teenagers do not feel comfortable talking about their problems.
4 It can be very frustrating for those what do not have any power.
5 People work with sick and elderly people must be very patient and kind.
6 People what continue to work after the age of 65 often live longer.
7 I understand that you mean.
8 The chart is on the left shows the number of students enrolled from 1999 to 2005.

8 How do I choose between *and, but* and *or*?

1 Tick the correct sentence in each pair.

1 a To really help the environment, we need to change the way we think or behave.
  b To really help the environment, we need to change the way we think and behave.
2 a Vegetarians don't eat meat and they get their protein from other foods.
  b Vegetarians don't eat meat but they get their protein from other foods.

We use *and* to join two similar ideas:
*Would you like some tea **and** biscuits?* (= you can have both of them)

We use *but* to show contrast between two different ideas:
*I have tea **but** I don't have any coffee, I'm afraid.* (I have tea = positive, I don't have any coffee = negative)

We use *or* to give an alternative:
*Would you like some tea **or** coffee?* (= you will choose only one of them)

☆ Note: to join two negative ideas, we use *or* if the subject and the verb are the same:
*I don't have tea **or** coffee.* (not: ~~I don't have tea and coffee.~~)
After *if / whether*, we can use *or not* to suggest the alternative idea:
*We decided to go whether it was raining **or not**.* (= whether it rained or whether it didn't rain)

2 Correct the mistake below.

Jenny loves the snow and James hates it.

Jenny loves the snow ....

3 Fill in the blanks with *and* / *but* / *or* / *or not*.

1 The town was quite small; it had no university .... college.
2 What shall we do tomorrow? We could go to the beach .... after that we could see a movie.
3 The number of people reaching the age of 100 .... more is increasing.
4 He had a computer, ... without a phone connection he couldn't access the internet.
5 It had black .... blue stripes on it – I can't remember which.
6 Do you know if our team won ....?
7 I enjoy playing football .... I don't really like watching it.
8 If you study in a country such as Australia, England .... America, your English will improve dramatically.

16

Auxiliary verbs

1 Tick the correct sentence in each pair.

1 a Why they think this?
  b Why do they think this?
2 a I am not agree with this idea.
  b I do not agree with this idea.

Do, *be* and *have* are called auxiliary verbs. This means that they help to change the main verb.

Do is used with the infinitive to make negatives or questions:
*I **don't** agree.* (not ~~I am not agree.~~) ***Do** you agree?* (not ~~Are you agree?~~)
Do can be used with other question words: *Why **do** you agree?* (not ~~Why you agree?~~)

Be is used with *-ing* verb forms to make the continuous tenses:
*I **am** study**ing** English in Cambridge.* (not ~~I studying English~~)
(*be* is also used with the past participle to make the passive – see unit 19)

Have is used with the past participle of the verb to make the perfect tenses:
*I **have been** here for three months.* (not ~~I am been here~~ or ~~I been here~~)

The auxiliary verb must agree with the subject of the verb (see unit 2): ***Does** your mother drink tea?* (not ~~Do your mother drink tea?~~)
☆ We make questions and negatives without *do* if another auxiliary verb is used:
***Are** you study**ing** here?* (not ~~Do you are studying here?~~) (auxiliary verb *be*)

2 Correct the mistakes below.

We going to play tennis.
Do you are want to join us?

We .... tennis. Do you ....?

3 Underline the correct auxiliary verb in each sentence. Sometimes no auxiliary is needed.

1 What *do* / *does* your friend like to eat?
2 Where *do* / *are* you going?
3 I *am* / *–* totally agree with you.
4 What *have* / *did* you done today?
5 I *am* / *do* not believe this.
6 She *is* / *are* learning the piano.
7 I *was* / *have* not seen her for two years.
8 They *–* / *are* went to America for their holiday.

17

Test 3

1 Complete sentences 1–8 using *and / but / or / or not* and a suitable ending from the box.

1 My grandfather doesn't have a DVD player ....
2 We swam in the sea ....
3 I enjoyed the walk ....
4 I couldn't decide whether ....
5 The tour fee includes all meals and transport ....
6 Nowadays, it is difficult to study without a computer ....
7 I like most drinks ....
8 The price for the hotel includes both breakfast ....

> ...I got a little lost near the end.   ...dinner.   ...not entry to the museum.
> ...I don't like coffee.   ...a laptop at home.   ...even a television at home.
> ...we walked along the beach collecting shells.   ...to go to the party.

2 Find and correct the 8 mistakes in the conversation below.

(C = customer, TA = travel agent)

C: Good morning. I'd like to book a holiday for myself and my family.

TA: Certainly, where would you like to go?

C: Well, I'd like to go for a week to an island somewhere with plenty to do, and I am not want to travel very far. Do you can suggest somewhere suitable?

TA: Well, there's a lovely island what is only two hours away by ferry.

C: That sounds good. Can I fly there?

TA: No, I'm afraid there don't any flights to the island.

C: I see. How much is it cost for a family of four?

TA: $1000.

C: Is that include the ferry?

TA: Yes, it includes all transport or hotel accommodation.

3 Add a relative pronoun to each of the following sentences. Which two sentences do not need a relative pronoun?

1 The students struggle the most are those without any maths qualifications.
2 It was my grandmother first taught me about art.
3 I'm not really sure we have to write about in this essay.
4 A thermometer is an instrument is used to measure temperature.
5 I am writing to apologise for I said to you last week.
6 Venus is a planet you can sometimes see without a telescope on a very clear night.
7 Yabbies are creatures live in rivers and lakes in Australia.
8 The people I know on my course are all from my previous school.

4 Fill in the blanks with the correct auxiliary verb: *be*, *do* or *have*.

1 What time .... you get home last night?
2 When .... you going to get a new car?
3 Where .... you been? I .... been waiting here for ages.
4 Stephen .... arriving on the 6 o'clock flight tomorrow morning.
5 A special tool .... used to cut the aluminium cans to the correct size.
6 .... not worry, I .... not going to tell your mother about your test result.
7 My sister wears very strange clothes; she .... not care what people think.
8 At last I .... finished my homework!

5 Fill in each blank in the following essay with one word.

Some people believe that too much money is spent on protecting animals and endangered species and that we should spend more money looking after the people on this planet instead. What are your views?

Whether you love animals (1).............. hate them, they play an important role in our ecosystem. Losing even a tiny insect species could have a very large impact on us all. For example, recent studies have shown that when there are fewer insects, there are also fewer birds. This means that crops will suffer because birds play an important role in pollinating plants, (2).............. they also eat insects that are harmful to plants.

Human beings are said to be the most dangerous animal on our planet, (3).............. we are also very vulnerable. If our crops fail, this could have disastrous consequences for all of us. In other words, we are as dependent on the tiny insects of this world as they are on us. They rely on us to protect them (4).............. their environment. If we do not, their numbers could begin to decline, (5).............. , even worse, they may become extinct altogether.

It is true that some people are already doing (6).............. they can to protect the environment, (7).............. this is not enough. Nowadays, people always want to buy the newest and latest gadgets, (8).............. what happens to the 'old' mobile phones, computers or toasters (9).............. are thrown away? We all need to realise that our everyday actions can have an impact on whether (10).............. not other animal species survive. We (11).............. need to stop buying new things altogether; however, we do need to change both the way we think (12).............. the way we behave.

10 How do I use modal verbs?

1 Tick the correct sentence in each pair.

1 a If workers are sick, they must to stay home and rest.
   b If workers are sick, they must stay home and rest.
2 a In this way, children can learn from what they have done.
   b In this way, children can learning from what they have done.

The following modal auxiliary verbs are followed by the infinitive without *to*: *can, could, may, might, must, shall, should, will, would*:
*When travelling, we **should respect** the customs of the countries we visit.* (not ~~should to respect; should respecting~~)

Modal verbs form questions and negatives without using *do*:
***Can** I **help** you?* (not: ~~Do I can help you?~~)
***Will** you **meet** me when I arrive?* (not ~~Do you will meet me~~)
*You **mustn't worry** about me.* (not ~~You do not must worry about me.~~)

When we talk about obligation or necessity using *have* or *need*, we use *to* + infinitive:
*I **have to finish** my assignment this weekend.*
*I **need to talk** to you.*
In questions and negatives, *have to* and *need to* behave like normal verbs and we use *do*:
***Do** you **have to pay** extra for breakfast?* (not ~~have you to pay~~)
*They said I **don't need to bring** my own sleeping bag.* (not ~~I needn't to bring~~)

2 Correct the mistake below.

You can't to smoking in this restaurant.

No Smoking

You ....

3 Correct the mistakes in the sentences below.

1 Nowadays, you can to find internet facilities in most hotels.
2 We do not should accept this situation any longer.
3 If we want to fix this problem, we must trying our best to change our attitude.
4 We haven't to stop using cars altogether but we do have to use them less often.
5 Do we can solve the problem of greenhouse gases in our lifetime?
6 Need you to take any food and drink with you, or are there shops there?
7 'Paula, you really must to study harder if you want to pass the exam.'
8 In my school, we have to left our mobile phones at home.

-ing or to + infinitive?

1 Tick the correct sentence in each pair.

1 a I just managed to avoid hitting the car in front of me.
  b I just managed to avoid to hit the car in front of me.
2 a I want telling you a little about myself.
  b I want to tell you a little about myself.

We use *to* + infinitive after the following verbs: *ask, afford, decide, deserve, help, hope, learn, offer, prepare, promise, refuse, seem, want, would like*:
Summer **seems to arrive** later and later these days.
Nowadays most people **would like to have** more money.
Learn how is also followed by *to* + infinitive:
I want to **learn how to drive** before I go to university.

After some verbs, we use *-ing*: *avoid, carry on, consider, deny, enjoy, finish, give up, imagine, involve, keep, like, mind, practise, recommend, resist, suggest*:
I really **enjoy watching** movies at the cinema. (not ~~enjoy to watch~~)
Look forward to is also followed by *-ing*:
I **look forward to hearing** your reply. (not ~~I look forward to hear your reply.~~)
We also use *-ing* after *spend money* and *spend time*:
We **spent a lot of money buying** CDs last month. We **spent $200 buying** CDs last month.
She **spent a lot of time looking** for information on the internet. She **spent over three hours looking** for information on the internet.
☆ Note that *like* can be followed by *-ing* or *to* + infinitive.

2 Correct the mistake below.

We've spent over $300 to buy food for the party.

We've spent ....

3 Fill in the gaps in the following sentences using the verb in brackets.

1 When I was a student, we couldn't afford .... new textbooks. (*buy*)
2 I was 13 when I first learnt how .... (*ice skate*)
3 What are you most looking forward to .... when your course finishes? (*do*)
4 'Keep .... the soup so that it doesn't stick to the bottom of the pan.' (*stir*)
5 My parents have promised .... me buy a car when I graduate. (*help*)
6 The children spent a long time .... the best present for their mother. (*choose*)
7 I've decided .... medicine at university. (*study*)
8 Our teacher suggested .... a barbecue on the last day of term. (*have*)

21

12 Verbs after adjectives and prepositions

1 Tick the correct sentence in each pair.

1 a Young children often feel shy to talk to adults.
  b Young children often feel shy talking to adults.
2 a It is easy to understand why.
  b It is easy understanding why.

With *feel* + adjective we use the *-ing* form of the verb:
*New students do not always **feel comfortable speaking** English to other people.*

After *be* + adjective, *too* + adjective and adjective + *enough*, we use *to* + infinitive:
*I **was happy to see** her when she arrived.* (not ~~I was happy seeing her~~)
*The lecture was **easy enough to understand**.* (not ~~enough easy~~ or ~~easy understanding~~)

After all prepositions (*about, by, from, for, in, of, without,* etc.) we use the *-ing* form of
the verb; we cannot use a clause (subject + verb):
*They celebrated their anniversary **by organising** a big party.*
*Thank you **for helping** me so much with my studies.*
*He opened the door **without thinking** about what would happen next.* (not ~~without he thought~~)

☆ Note that *despite, in spite of* and *instead of* are considered to be prepositions:
*He did not get the job **despite getting** excellent grades.* (not ~~despite he got~~)
*She went to the library **instead of going** straight home after school.* (not ~~instead of she went~~)

If the following verb is negative, we use *not* + *-ing*: *He got a job **despite not getting** good grades.*

2 Correct the mistake below.

Alice won the tournament
in spite of she was the
youngest player.

Alice won the tournament ....

3 Underline the correct word or phrase in the sentences below.

1 It was easy *understanding / to understand* why they liked living close to the beach.
2 When they finally arrived, the students were too tired *cooking / to cook* anything.
3 I felt very nervous *presenting / to present* my assignment to the class.
4 The large tree prevented them from *getting / to get* wet in the rain.
5 I'm sorry for *causing / to cause* you so much trouble.
6 The lady in front was wearing a hat that was too big *seeing / to see* over.
7 They still couldn't afford the hotel in spite of *receiving / they received* a 10% discount.
8 They decided to rent a flat instead of *staying / to stay* in a hotel.

Test 4

1 Complete the questions and answers using the words in brackets.

A: (1) .... stamps at the newsagent's? (*can/buy*)

B: (2) .... to the post office. (*Yes/can. Not/have to/go*)

A: (3) .... our assignment in this Friday? (*have to/hand*)

B: (4) .... it in until the following week. (*No/not have to/give*)

A: (5) .... the test on Saturday? (*need to/Joe/take*)

B: (6) Yes, so .... to the party on Friday. (*should/not/go*)

2 Join the two sentences together using the words in brackets.

1 They went to the cinema. They didn't go to school. (*instead of*)
   ....

2 I enjoyed the party. I did not know anyone there. (*despite*)
   ....

3 I am optimistic about the future. There are so many problems in the world. (*in spite of*)
   ....

4 We all enjoyed the course. We had to work so hard. (*despite*)
   ....

5 My parents gave me some money. They didn't buy me a present. (*instead of*)
   ....

6 The company went out of business. They spent thousands of dollars on marketing. (*in spite of*)
   ....

3 Find 12 mistakes with *to* in the candidate's answers. You may need to add *to* or delete it.

Interviewer: What kind of thing do you like doing in your spare time?

Candidate: Well, I really enjoy to listening to music and I also like doing sport in my free time. I think everyone should to look after their body and try keep fit. I love soccer, and I was actually offered a place in my local soccer team, but I had turn it down because my parents wouldn't to allow me take it.

Interviewer: Are there any new skills you would like to learn in the future?

Candidate: Well, as I said, I love music, so I would love to learn to play the guitar one day. When I was younger, my parents suggested to studying a musical instrument, but I wasn't interested at that time. If you want be a good musician, you really must to work hard and keep to practising every day. At that time, I was spending a lot of time to studying so I couldn't do it then, but I'm looking forward learning to play some time in the future.

4 Fill in the blanks with the correct form of the verbs in the box.

| get | make | practise | show | speak (× 3) | study | waste |

Welcome to our school. I am the principal of the college and I'd just like to say a few words while your teacher is preparing (1)........................... you a short video about our lovely town. We are all very pleased that you have decided (2)........................... at our college. Some of you are here for only a few weeks, so you can't afford (3)........................... any time in your studies. Learning (4)........................... any language involves (5)........................... that language as much as possible. So from today, I recommend (6)........................... only English. While you are here, you should consider (7)........................... as many friends as possible from other countries so that you don't spend too much time (8)........................... your own language. Well, I think the video is ready now. I hope (9)........................... the opportunity to meet you all individually at lunch.

5 Fill in the blanks using the words in brackets.

1 I didn't mind washing the dishes. I was .... (*happy / do*) it.
2 Your essay was .... (*impossible / mark*) because the handwriting was .... (*too / difficult / understand*).
3 Alex felt .... (*excited / get*) ready for the party.
4 I'm renting a flat because it was .... (*too / expensive / buy*) one.
5 Our team was just .... (*not / fit / enough / win*) the match.
6 There is so much bad news that I often feel .... (*sad / watch*) the news on TV.

The gerund or infinitive after *allow, advise, make, suggest*?

1 Tick the correct sentence in each pair.

1 a My school does not allow us taking holidays during term.
  b My school does not allow us to take holidays during term.
2 a Our teacher suggested me to buy a good dictionary.
  b Our teacher suggested I buy a good dictionary.

Some verbs are followed by *-ing* if there is no object and by *to* + infinitive if there is a direct object – *advise, allow, forbid, permit*:
*The teacher **allowed talking** as long as it was in English.* (no direct object)
*The teacher **allowed us to talk** as long as it was in English.* (*us* is the direct object)

Make is followed by the infinitive without *to*:
*My boss **made me wear** a horrible uniform.* (not ~~made me to wear~~)
☆ Note that the direct object must come between the verb and the infinitive:
*She **allowed her dog to sit** in the front of her car.* (not ~~She allowed to sit her dog~~)

In the passive, these verbs are followed by *to* + infinitive: *be advised, be allowed, be forbidden, be made, be permitted*:
*I **was advised to contact** my travel agent as soon as the plane landed.*
*Mary **was made to swallow** a large dose of medicine by the nurse.*

Suggest can be followed by *-ing* without a direct object:
*John **suggested going** to a movie.*
If there is a direct object, you can use the infinitive without *to*, or a *that* clause:
*John **suggested we go** to a movie.* or: *John **suggested that we go** to a movie.*

2 Correct the mistake below.

You're not allowed to skateboarding in the park.

You're ....

3 Correct the mistakes in the sentences below.

1 I suggest you going and doing your homework now if you want to watch TV later.
2 My parents always made me to clean up my room when I was young.
3 I think people should not be allowed using mobile phones in the cinema.
4 Nowadays it is forbidden smoking in many restaurants and public areas.
5 After a lot of effort, I finally made work my new DVD player.
6 The police advised local residents not to leaving their windows open at night.
7 This ticket will permit that you enter the museum as many times as you like.
8 Our teacher suggested to go to the park for our end-of-term party.

Stop, try, forget and remember

1 Tick the correct sentence in each pair.

1 a People should stop spending their money on the latest fashions.
   b People should stop to spend their money on the latest fashions.
2 a The government tried stopping this plan but was not successful.
   b The government tried to stop this plan but was not successful.

Some verbs have a different meaning when they are followed by *-ing* or *to* + infinitive.

Stop + *-ing* = to stop an activity. *Stop* + *to* + infinitive = to stop a previously mentioned activity in order to do something else. Compare:
*The boys **stopped playing**.*
*The boys were playing and they **stopped to watch** a large truck go past.* (= they stopped playing in order to watch the truck)

Try + *-ing* = to attempt to solve a problem by doing something. *Try* + *to* + infinitive = to attempt and fail to do something. Compare:
*I **tried turning** the tap but the water still poured out.* (I managed to turn the tap)
*I **tried to turn** the tap but it was too old and rusty.* (I couldn't turn the tap)

Forget / remember + *-ing* = thinking back to a special/significant time in the past.
Forget / remember + *to* + infinitive = thinking about something that must be done in the future. Compare:
*I **remember seeing** a bull running down the High Street.* (this happened in the past)
*I must **remember to watch** the news tonight.* (first I must remember, then I will do it)

2 Correct the mistake below.

I lost the race because I had to stop tying my shoelace.

I lost the race because ....

3 Fill in the blanks with the correct form of the verb in brackets.

1 Nowadays many people want to stop .... too hard and enjoy life. (*work*)
2 Did you remember .... candles for the birthday cake? (*buy*)
3 The burglar tried .... the window with a knife but couldn't get in. (*open*)
4 Don't forget .... a postcard to your grandmother when you're away. (*send*)
5 At 12 o'clock every day the builders stopped .... a lunch break. (*have*)
6 I will never forget .... the pyramids on our trip to Egypt. (*visit*)
7 The cook tried .... more salt but the soup was still too bland. (*add*)
8 I remember .... across the road but I have no idea how I ended up in hospital. (*walk*)

Prepositions after adjectives and nouns

1 Tick the correct sentence in each pair.

1 a My brother is good at sport but he is very bad at English.
  b My brother is good in sport but he is very bad in English.
2 a The percentage in women attending university is increasing.
  b The percentage of women attending university is increasing.

Some adjectives are always followed by a specific preposition.
At. We say you are *bad at, good at* or *surprised at* something:
*I was **surprised at** the number of people who came.*
About and ***with***. We say you are *angry about* or *pleased about* something but *angry with* or *pleased with* a person:
*I am **pleased about** your new job. I was really **angry with** John.*
After *disappointed* we use *about* or *with*; after *worried* we only use *about*:
*She was pretty **disappointed with / about** her exam results.*
*I am **worried about** John. They are **worried about** the test.*

Some nouns are always followed by a specific preposition.
In. We say *decrease in, drop in, fall in, increase in, rise in*:
*There was an **increase in** attendance at this month's meeting.*
Between. To contrast two things, we talk about the *difference between* them:
*The main **difference between** the American and the Canadian accent is in the vowels.*
Of. We say: *advantage of, disadvantage of, example of, number of, percentage of, use of*:
*The **number of** people in my class who smoke is incredible.*

2 Correct the mistake below.

The class look very pleased of their final results.

The class look ....

3 Fill in the blanks using a word from this unit and the correct preposition.

1 I've never been very .... painting or drawing.
2 The USA's population is far greater, so there is a big .... the two totals.
3 One .... saving money is that you will be able to enjoy your retirement.
4 The most dramatic .... numbers occurred in 1997, with a 30% rise.
5 Peter was very .... robotics, so he enjoyed the lecture very much.
6 The .... children with obesity problems is increasing each year.
7 One .... multi-tasking is reading emails while talking on the phone.
8 Fortunately, there was a steady .... the number of road accidents.

1 Fill in the blanks using the correct form of the verbs in the box.

bring	borrow	complete	copy	email	reserve	store	use

Library Rules

- Students are allowed (1)........................ up to six items at a time.
- It is forbidden (2)........................ food or drink into the library at any time.
- Students are advised (3)........................ valuables in the lockers provided.
- Some library resources are very popular at exam times. We advise (4)........................ a copy of any material you will need well in advance.
- Although we do allow students (5)........................ library materials, we remind all students to pay careful attention to the copyright information posted near the photocopying machines.
- The library allows (6)........................ on certain computers; however, to ensure access for all students, you are not permitted (7)........................ the computers without making a booking at the information desk.
- The library closes at 9:00 pm. We suggest (8)........................ any transactions at least 10 minutes before this time.

2 Find the 8 places in the text where you need to add a preposition.

The chart shows the number people moving between the villages in the south and the cities in the north in recent years. The main difference the two sets of figures is that the percentage people living in the south is decreasing steadily, while there has been a rise population figures for the northern cities. The biggest increase population in the northern cities occurred in 2001, and this corresponds with the biggest decrease the number people living in the southern villages. Since 2002, the number inhabitants in both the north and the south has remained steady.

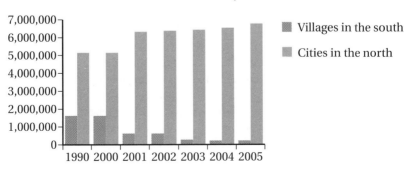

■ Villages in the south

■ Cities in the north

3 Underline the correct word or phrase in these sentences.

1 I was very bad *at/in* sports when I was at school.
2 Is it possible to make people *give up/to give up* smoking?
3 I stopped *working/to work* to listen to the news.
4 I was surprised *at/of* how calm I felt before the performance.
5 I'll never forget *coming/to come* first in the race.
6 I was talking on the phone, but I stopped *answering/to answer* the door.
7 My teacher was very pleased *for/with* my exam results.
8 Remember *brushing/to brush* your teeth every morning and night.

4 A teacher has underlined 14 mistakes in this essay. Correct the mistakes for the student.

Smoking causes many health problems, is a drain on the workforce and is very expensive. Clearly, there are many good reasons (1) to stop people to smoke.

First, we need to ask ourselves whether this is the responsibility of the government. As we can see, this problem has an impact on (2) many areas our life. (3) One important example for this is the economy. If people spend too much money on cigarettes, they will not save as much money for their future. Furthermore, if they become ill, the government will need to take care of them. I believe the government does have a duty to educate people about (4) the disadvantages for smoking and we should all (5) be worried for this problem. However, it is not enough just to (6) advise people to not smoking.

So, what can governments do? Some governments have already (7) tried to increase the tax on tobacco, but even though cigarettes are expensive, people still buy them. Governments have also (8) tried finding ways to target cigarette manufacturers without success. In my country, we only (9) allow to smoke in our own homes and (10) people are not permitted smoking in restaurants or bars. I believe this is an effective way to (11) make people to stop smoking or at least to reduce (12) the number cigarettes they smoke.

(13) I suggest all governments to adopt this strategy. In this way we may also (14) prevent more children to take up this unhealthy habit.

16 Prepositions after verbs

1 Tick the correct sentence in each pair.

1 a The company agreed for the pay rise.
   b The company agreed to the pay rise.
2 a The man apologised for standing on my foot.
   b The man apologised to stand on my foot.

Some verbs must be followed by a specific preposition. Sometimes more than one preposition is possible and sometimes there is a difference in meaning depending on which preposition is used:

Agree. We say you *agree with* a person or an idea:
*I totally **agree with** the government's decision.*
But if you give your consent to something, we use *agree to*:
*Both sides in the war have **agreed to** the ceasefire.*
Apologise. We say you *apologise to* someone but you *apologise for* something:
*Mum made me go and **apologise to** our neighbours **for** breaking their window.*
Find out, know, learn, teach, think. These verbs can all be followed by *about*:
*Our teacher is trying to **teach** us **about** life in the olden days.*
Think can be followed by *about* or *of* to talk about opinions or future plans:
*What do you **think about** / **of** the new computer lab?* (opinion)
*I'm **thinking about** / **of** going back to university next year to finish my degree.* (future plan)
Look. We use *look at* when we fix our eyes on something and *look for* when we mean searching for something:
*Oh **look at** the sunset! Isn't it beautiful?*
*I've **looked for** my homework everywhere. Have you seen it?*

2 Correct the mistake below.

> I spend a lot of time looking at my car keys.

I spend a lot of time ....

3 Fill in the blanks using the correct preposition.

1 I don't know very much .... ancient history.
2 The manager agreed .... an increase in staff holidays.
3 The airline apologised .... losing my luggage.
4 How did you find out .... our college?
5 What are you thinking .... doing in the school holidays?
6 We went to the zoo because I wanted to look .... the penguins.
7 I agree .... the teacher – you really need to improve your handwriting.
8 'What are you looking ....?' 'My glasses, I can't find them anywhere.'

Prepositions of time and place

1 Tick the correct sentence in each pair.

1   a   I will start my course on June.

      b   I will start my course in June.

2   a   I am going in London next year.

      b   I am going to London next year.

We use *in* with a year, month or part of the day, but *on* with a day or date:
*I came to Australia **in 1988**. We landed **on 1st October, in the afternoon**.*
We use *at* with a time and with *the weekend* and *night*:
*Let's meet **at the weekend**. Are you free on Sunday **at 8:00**?*
We use *for* to talk about a length of time:
*I have lived in Australia **for 18 years**.*

We use *in* with cities, countries and places to say where something is or happened:
*I met my husband **in London**.*
We also use *in* with a book, newspaper, magazine, journal, film or TV programme to say where we read or saw something:
*I read some interesting new research **in** this month's medical **journal**.*

We use *at* with *school, college, university, work* and *home* and to refer to a building:
*'Where is dad?' 'He's **at work**.'*
*Shall we meet **at the cinema**?* (= meet outside the building)

We use *to* with a place to show destination:
*'Where are you going?' 'I'm just going **to the library** to do some work.'*

2 Correct the mistake below.

I'll have to walk at work during the train strike.

I'll have to ....

3 Fill in the blanks using the correct preposition.

1   I started high school .... 1985.

2   Shall we meet .... the library and then go in together?

3   I have been studying English .... 3 years.

4   I was born .... June 17th 1991.

5   Pete and Jane go .... Australia next week. They are going to study .... Sydney.

6   The movie starts .... 7:30 so we'll need to get there before then.

7   That actor was much younger .... the movie we saw last night.

8   I find that I do my best work .... night.

18 The preposition *of*

1 Tick the correct sentence in each pair.

1 a *Our standard of living is much better than in the past.*
  b *Our standard for living is much better than in the past.*
2 a *Write a letter complaint to the manager.*
  b *Write a letter of complaint to the manager.*

The preposition *of* is used in some common expressions: *cost of living, letter of apology/complaint,* etc., *period of time, quality of life, standard of living*:
*My father is always complaining about the high **cost of living** nowadays.*

Of is also used after some nouns: *government, group, importance, lack, leader, type*:
*People often underestimate the **importance of** friends and family.*

Of is used to talk about quantities with some words: *amount, number, a lot, lots, plenty*:
*The government is hoping to persuade a large **number of** people to walk to work.*

Of is used in some prepositions: *in front of, instead of*:
*I decided to take the bus **instead of** the train.*

Also after *because* and *as a result* when they are followed by a noun or gerund:
*My cousin couldn't swim with us **because of** his bad leg.* (not ~~because his bad leg~~)
*Our football team was demoted **as a result of the weather being bad**.* (not ~~as a result of the weather was bad~~)

2 Correct the mistake below.

There is a bus stop in front the post office.

There is a bus stop ....

3 Correct the mistakes in the following sentences. There may be more than one mistake in some sentences.

1 It is difficult for very old people to have a good quality for life.
2 The lakes remained empty for a long period time during the drought.
3 I missed out on a good job promotion as a result my illness.
4 The government for my country tries to consult everyone about important issues.
5 I wrote a letter complaint to the airline because they lost my luggage.
6 There are a large number different types cars on our roads nowadays.
7 The leader for the opposition was very angry with the result at the election.
8 We ate at home instead to go to a restaurant because we couldn't decide what type food we wanted.

Test 6

1 This is a talk to high school students. Fill in the blanks using the correct form of one of the verbs in the box, and a preposition.

| agree | find out | know | look (× 2) | teach | think |

It's that time of year again when our final-year students start to (1)............................ university and all of the decisions that need to be made before then. Your teachers felt that you needed some advice on this subject and I quite (2)............................ them, so I have come along today to do just that. First, talk to your teachers. Not only do they (3)............................ (*you*) their subjects, but they can also give you some very useful advice about your strengths and weaknesses. Secondly, make a list of what you already (4)............................ university study. That will help you pinpoint what you still need to (5)............................ . The internet can be an invaluable tool, but there is little point in searching for information if you don't know what you are (6)............................ , otherwise you can waste hours of valuable study time just (7)............................ the computer screen.

2 Correct the mistakes in the following sentences.

1 I agree to what you are saying, but I think there is another side to the argument.
2 The difference with your essay and mine is that I only answered part of the question.
3 Our teacher stressed the importance to checking our writing for spelling mistakes.
4 Fruit bats emerge in night to feed on the many fruit trees in the area.
5 Can you meet me tomorrow morning in 10:00?
6 I've been working in this coffee shop in six months.
7 My birthday is in 8th November; when is yours?
8 Alex started piano lessons on July last year.

3 Add the correct prepositions to the following conversation.

Mary: Thanks for coming everyone. As you know, Sue, our receptionist is off sick and it may be some time before she's back (1)............. work. I'll have a replacement tomorrow, but today we'll all need to help out.

Tom: Well, I teach (2)............. the afternoons, but I could cover reception (3)............. an hour this morning. I just need to make sure I have time to prepare for my presentation (4)............. the university (5)............. 17th June.

Mary: OK, I'll put you down for 9:00 to 10:00. What about you Margaret?

Margaret: Actually, I can do a couple of hours this afternoon because I managed to get a lot of work done (6)............. the weekend. I've promised to take my class to see a play (7)............. Friday, so I really need to get that organised this morning.

Mary: That's fine. I did have a meeting (8)............. the city (9)............. 11:00 but I can cancel that and cover (10)............. three hours from 10:00 to 1:00 myself. Well done, everyone! Thank you.

4 Underline the correct answer.

1 I quite agree *to* / *with* you.
2 'What's Ann doing?' 'She's looking *at* / *for* her passport.'
3 I must apologise *for* / *to* being late; my car broke down.
4 After a few hours, mum finally agreed *to* / *with* take us to the movies.
5 I stopped at the shops on the way home *because* / *because of* I needed some milk.
6 'Where's Bill?' 'He's at the art gallery looking *at* / *for* the paintings.'
7 Tim and Bob couldn't go to the party *because* / *because of* their tennis match.
8 I apologised *for* / *to* everyone when my phone rang during the meeting.

5 Complete the letter using the information from the notes.

Problem ⟶	Reason
rooms were noisy	the hotel wasn't finished
couldn't use the pool	the water was so dirty
son cut his foot	he swam at the beach
trip to Mt Etna spoiled	the weather was so bad
couldn't see the top of the mountain	it was covered by cloud
missed part of the show	the bus broke down
wife sick	she ate undercooked chicken

Dear Sir

I am writing to complain about a recent holiday I took with your company.

First, our accommodation was terrible. It was very noisy as a result of (1).......................... , so builders were working on it day and night. Not only that, but we couldn't use the pool because of (2)........................... . We would have liked to go to the beach more often, but on the first day my son cut his foot badly as a result of (3)........................... in the sea there, and we discovered there was a lot of broken glass in the sand.

Secondly, we paid a great deal of money for two trips. The first one to Mt Etna was ruined because of (4)........................... . In fact we couldn't even see the top of the mountain because of (5)........................... . The second trip was to a show in the local town. However, we missed the start of the show as a result of (6)........................... on the way there. Furthermore, my wife ended up in hospital as a result of (7)........................... at the restaurant there.

I would be grateful if you could refund the cost of our trip.

Yours faithfully

Fraser Cullen

19 How do I make a verb passive?

1 Tick the correct sentence in each pair.

1 a My home is located in the western part of the city.
 b My home locates in the western part of the city.
2 a These funds can be give to the poorer people to help them.
 b These funds can be given to the poorer people to help them.

The passive is formed with the verb *to be* + the past participle of the verb:
*Nowadays, a great deal of money **is spent** on advertising.*

The verb *to be* should be changed into the correct tense:

Tense	Passive
present simple	*is spent*
present continuous	*is being spent*
simple past	*was spent*
past continuous	*was being spent*
present perfect	*has been spent*
past perfect	*had been spent*

To make the negative, we put *not* between the verb *to be* and the past participle:
*We **were not told** that the rules had changed.*
The passive can also be used in the infinitive form:
*Children need **to be taught** the correct way to behave in public.*

After modal verbs, we use the passive infinitive without *to*:
*Some adults believe that children **should be seen** and not **heard**.*
*You **will be paid** on the last Friday of each month.*

2 Correct the mistake below.

I gave this painting by my grandmother.

I ....

3 Correct the mistakes in the following sentences. You do not need to change the tense.

1 The house was sell for over one million dollars.
2 The class has allowed to eat in the staff dining room during the renovations.
3 The potatoes carry along a conveyor belt to a room where they wash and peel.
4 The teacher told to take her class out of the school if the fire bell rang.
5 Smoking do not allow in any part of the aeroplane.
6 The museum was being renovating when we were there, so we could not visit it.
7 Bus tickets can buy at any newsagents.
8 New employees have instructed not to operate the photocopier until they are trained.

When do I use the passive?

1 Tick the correct sentence in each pair.

1 a Many people have been died because of this disease.
   b Many people have died because of this disease.
2 a This data took from 1982 and 1992.
   b This data was taken from 1982 and 1992.

With active verbs we usually use the following order: subject + verb + object. We use the passive when we want to put the object of the verb first: object + verb. Compare:
*The **teacher told the students** to close their books.* = active (subject + verb + object)
*The **students were told** to close their books.* = passive (object + verb)

We use the passive:
- when we want to make the object the focus of the sentence: ***The books were sold*** *for a small profit at the school.* (the focus is on the books, not the person selling them)
☆ Note that the verb (*were*) agrees with the object (*the books*).
- when the context tells us who carried out the action: ***A law was introduced*** *to help protect people in this situation.* (we know that the government did this)
- when it is not important who carried out the action: *In the factory, **the shoes are cleaned** and **packed** into boxes ready for sale.* (we do not need to know who does this)
☆ Note that we can include the 'subject' by adding *by* + the person/group: *A lot of waste materials could be recycled **by large manufacturers**.*

2 Correct the mistake below.

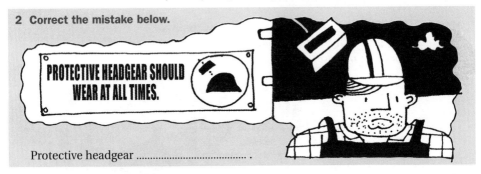

PROTECTIVE HEADGEAR SHOULD WEAR AT ALL TIMES.

Protective headgear ....

3 Change the following sentences from active to passive. You will not need to change the tense. You will need to decide when to leave out the subject.

1 A factory worker checks each box for quality. *Each box* ....
2 The government does not permit children under 16 to work. *Children* ....
3 The washing machine is washing your clothes at the moment. *Your clothes* ....
4 A mechanic will repair your car this afternoon. *Your car* ....
5 The agent has sold our house at last. *Our house* ....
6 Something tore the back of my coat. *The back of my coat* ....
7 The employer pays the staff more for working at the weekend. *The staff* ....
8 Burning tyres give off highly toxic chemicals. *Highly toxic chemicals* ....

What is register?

1 Tick the correct sentence in each pair.

1 a This type of work attracts a greater % of men than women.
   b This type of work attracts a greater percentage of men than women.
2 a Many old people believe that kids have too much freedom nowadays.
   b Many old people believe that children have too much freedom nowadays.

'Register' means using the right word in the right context. For formal essay writing, you must use a formal register. This means you should not use informal language. You should not use:

• informal vocabulary: not *kids*; *ok*; *bucks*; *heaps*. You should use a more formal equivalent instead: *children*; *all right* or *acceptable*; *money*; *many* or *a great deal*.

• symbols on their own in place of words: not *%*; *$*; *&*; *@*. You should write the words in full: *percent*; *money*; *and*; *at*. Note that *%* and *$* should only be used with numerals. For smaller amounts we write *$50* (not *50 dollars*) and *75%* (not *75 percent*). The noun form of *percent* is *percentage*.

• abbreviations: not *m*; *yrs*; *kgs*; *no*. You should write these words in full: *million*; *years*; *kilos/kilograms*; *number*.

• all capital letters: not NOWADAYS PEOPLE THINK THAT... You should use capital letters only when appropriate: *Nowadays people think that...*

Look at the following examples:
Companies waste ~~heaps of bucks~~ on advertising. → *waste **a great deal of money** on...*
In 1986 the ~~%~~ rose to 67.5. → *the **percentage** rose to...*
Between the ~~yrs~~ 2001 and 2005, over ~~2m~~ people died. → *the **years**... over **2 million**...*

2 Correct the mistake below.

The new hospital cost over 200 million bucks to build.

HOSPITAL

NEWS

The new hospital ....

3 Correct the register errors in the following sentences. There may be more than one.

1 Some people believe it is ok to hit small children.
2 Kids today are much more comfortable using technology than older people.
3 The no. of people without a job in the yr 2001 was 3.5m.
4 The government needs to create heaps of jobs to solve this problem.
5 A LARGE AMOUNT OF $ IS SPENT ON DEVELOPING TOURISM.
6 The female employees tend to go out more during their lunch break than the guys.
7 35% of students agreed with the decision but the % that disagreed was far greater.
8 The baby blue whale gains 90 kgs per day.

1 Match the people or group to the correct sentence.

> the burglar   the government   the hospital staff   the nation
> the principal   the waiter

1 The main dish was served on a silver platter. ......*the waiter*....
2 Each year the most improved student is chosen. ....
3 A new law has been passed to make the dumping of waste illegal. ....
4 I realised my keys had been stolen during the break-in. ....
5 Simon is being treated for minor burns. ....
6 Our new government will be elected on June 20th. ....

Now rewrite the sentences in the active using the subjects from the box.

1 *The waiter served the main dish on a silver platter.*...
2 ....
3 ....
4 ....
5 ....
6 ....

2 Find 10 verbs that should be in the passive and make the necessary changes.

How to train your new puppy

There are two main types of training: behavioural and obedience.
Behavioural training should do on a one-to-one basis. This type of training
uses to correct any bad habits your dog may have developed, such as
climbing on furniture. Obedience training should do often but only for short periods of time. It is
best to train your dog just before meals so his meal associates with a reward for the training.

It is important to keep your puppy safe from danger. Many young puppies injure because
their owners don't realise how curious they can be. One way to protect your puppy is by
giving him a special house. The house can make of any suitable material but it must be big
enough for the puppy to move around comfortably. It can use for house-training your puppy
or to protect him from very young children.

You should never try to win your puppy's affection by allowing him to do what he likes. If
your puppy rewards with a cuddle and a pat when he jumps on the furniture, then he will
continue to do this. To correct jumping, first your puppy's feet should place firmly back on
the floor. Then the puppy gives a treat when he is on the floor. It is important to make sure
that other people know they cannot pet him or reward him if he jumps up.

3 Fill in the gaps in the following paragraph using the information in the diagrams.

How to make a traditional canoe

1 Choose a suitable tree. 2 Strip the bark. 3 Soak the bark.

4 Heat the bark over a fire. Do not allow it to burn. 5 Place the bark between trees to shape it. 6 Sew the edges together.

7 You have finished your canoe. 8 Indigenous people use them to catch fish.

The diagrams show how a traditional canoe (1)......................... . First, a suitable tree (2)......................... and then the bark (3)......................... off in one piece. Next, the bark (4)......................... in a river so that it becomes soft and pliable. It (5).........................
(*then*) over a fire but it should (6)......................... (*not*) to burn. In order to shape the bark, it should (7)......................... between two trees that are growing close together. Finally, once the bark has cooled, the edges (8)......................... together. Your canoe (9)......................... . These canoes (10)......................... for fishing.

4 Correct the 10 mistakes in the following text.

The graph shows the no. of people who shop online and the types of stuff that bought. It is clear that most money spend on travel and accommodation, and the smallest amount of money is spending on groceries. The first figures available are for the yr 1995, because shopping online was not common before then. The % of people shopping online was very small initially, and it took ages for people to begin using this service. However, the majority of people still wanna visit shops in person to do their shopping, and only 20% of the population say they have ever bought anything online. Of the 20% who have used online shopping, 75% say they have been received good value for money and they would definitely use it again.

Adjectives and adverbs

1 Tick the correct sentence in each pair.

1 a This difference can be explained quite easy.

   b This difference can be explained quite easily.

2 a It is clearly that people without money do not have as much freedom.

   b It is clear that people without money do not have as much freedom.

Adjectives are used to describe a noun: *Today **life** is very **complicated**.* (*complicated* describes the noun *life*)

To describe a whole idea or situation, we can use *It is* + adjective + *that*-clause or *It is* + adjective + *to* + infinitive:

***It is essential that** you bring back all of your books before the end of term.*

***It is important to begin** studying several weeks before the exam.*

Adverbs can be used to describe a verb: *We must **act quickly**.* (*quickly* describes the verb *act*) or an adjective: *This chart is **significantly different**.* (not ~~significant different~~) (*significantly* is an adverb describing the adjective *different*).

We use adverbs such as *unfortunately* to show how we feel about something:

***Unfortunately**, he's not well.* (*unfortunately* shows I feel this is a bad thing)

☆ Some adverbs are irregular, e.g. *fast, hard, well*: *He ran as **fast** as he could.* (not ~~fastly~~)

2 Correct the mistake below.

Michael's studying hardly for his exams.

Michael's studying ....

3 Underline the correct words.

1 I didn't play very *good / well* in our last football match.

2 In 1980, this figure increased *sharp / sharply* to 75%.

3 There was a *gradual / gradually* increase in numbers between 1990 and 1995.

4 It is *clear / clearly* that people with experience can find a job more *easy / easily*.

5 I *strong / strongly* agree with this point of view.

6 *Severe / Severely* punishments may not help to reduce crime.

7 *Unfortunate / Unfortunately*, I am unable to attend the meeting this Saturday.

8 It is *vital / vitally* important to address these problems before it is too late.

Noun or adjective?

1 Tick the correct sentence in each pair.

1 a Tourism can be very benefit to poorer areas.
  b Tourism can be very beneficial to poorer areas.
2 a In my job, you need the confidence to address large groups of people.
  b In my job, you need the confident to address large groups of people.

Sometimes it is easy to confuse a noun with its adjective. Look at the following list of commonly confused nouns and adjectives:

Noun	Adjective	Noun	Adjective
age	*aged*	*noise*	*noisy*
development	*developed*	*responsibility*	*responsible*
difference	*different*	*significance*	*significant*
education	*educational*	*silence*	*silent*
happiness	*happy*	*sport*	*sports*
health	*healthy*	*truth*	*true*
maturity	*mature*	*value*	*valuable*
nature	*natural*	*youth*	*young*

☆ Note that *invaluable* means very valuable!
☆ *Men* and *women* can only be used as nouns: *More **men** than **women** work here.*
Male and *female* are used as adjectives: *The number of **female** employees is increasing each year.* (not ~~women employees~~)
You should refer to either *men* and *women* or *male* and *female*. Do not use the two different terms together: ~~Male employees far outnumber the women.~~

2 Correct the mistake below.

I'm looking for a ....

I'm looking for a good pair of sport shoes.

3 Correct the mistakes in the sentences below.

1 I can't tell the different between the fake designer goods and the real ones.
2 The advice my tutor gave me was unvaluable in the exam.
3 It is important to eat a health diet when you are studying or exercising hard.
4 In some countries, there are no women members of parliament.
5 I can't study in silent; I need to have music in the background.
6 A child who is loved is a happiness child.
7 Both women and males need to be included in these decisions.
8 The landlord complained because we were making too much noisy.

Verb confusion 1 – courses and study

1 Tick the correct sentence in each pair.

1 a I don't know where the library is.

  b I don't understand where the library is.

2 a Last summer I studied with you on the course.

  b Last summer I learned with you on the course.

- *Know* is used to show that you have memorised something or that you are certain of something: *I know all of the irregular verbs. Know* describes a state, not an activity (not ~~I am trying to know my irregular verbs.~~) and we cannot use it in the continuous form (not ~~I am knowing my irregular verbs.~~).

- *Learn* describes an activity. We *learn* facts when we try to memorise them: *I am **learning** irregular verbs for the test.* We can also *learn* a skill: *I am **learning** to play the piano.* We cannot use *learn* by itself (not ~~I am learning for the test.~~)

- *Study* is usually used to talk about a whole subject area rather than individual skills or facts: *My daughter is **studying** economics at university* (not ~~I am studying how to play the piano.~~). We can use *study* by itself: *I am **studying** for the test on Friday.* Note that we can say *learn about* but not *study about*: *We're **learning about** World War I this term.* (not ~~we're studying about~~).

- *Take* can be used in a similar way to *study* to refer to a subject area: *I am **taking** a course in marketing.* It is also used to refer to the individual subjects within a course: *I have to **take** at least 3 marketing subjects to get the diploma.*

- *Enrol* is used to say that you are listed in the official records for a course. *I have just **enrolled** in an art course.*

2 Correct the mistake below.

We would like ....

3 Choose the correct verb to complete the sentences below.

1 We're *learning / studying* about Ancient Rome this term.

2 I've decided to *enrol in / learn* a photography course this summer.

3 I can hum the tune but I don't *know / learn* the words.

4 In high school you *know / study* many different subjects.

5 Before you can fly a plane, you need to *learn / study* how to land.

6 Jane is *learning / studying* in London this year.

7 Do you *know / learn* the telephone number for the school?

8 I can't go out on Friday. I have to *learn / study* for my end-of-year exams.

Test 8

1 **Fill in the blanks in the sentences below using the correct form of one of the words in the box.**

> benefit   confident   develop   different   health   nature   responsible
> significant

1 I didn't have the .... to join the school debating team.
2 We hope this new source of power will lead to the .... of new businesses in our area.
3 There is a great deal of evidence that a diet of fast food is not ....
4 If you make a mistake, it is important to take .... for your actions.
5 At first Joe didn't realise the .... of his discovery.
6 It was almost impossible to tell the .... between the twins.
7 In some ways, it is better to use .... ingredients like sugar and butter rather than manufactured foods.
8 Studies have shown that exercising three times a week is .... for the heart.

2 **Correct the 8 mistakes in the following text.**

Teacher   Why do you think that education has become so important nowadays?

Student   Well, I think people are more concern these days about being success in their career. And nowadays you really have to be very well education if you want to get a good job. Our life is also more competition these days, so you have to study hardly at school and university. I think good qualifications can make a big different in getting the job you want. You also need to be able to speak English good, so it's importance to study languages as well as other subjects.

3 **Complete the following sentences using the correct form of the words in brackets.**

1 The figures in the two charts are .... different. (*significant*)
2 In 2002 the number of houses sold increased .... (*slight*)
3 These figures fell .... in 2005. (*sharp*)
4 The concert was .... noisy. (*incredible*)
5 .... , we didn't get to see the Eiffel Tower on our trip. (*sad*)
6 The lecture on robotics was .... interesting. (*extreme*)
7 The number of students enrolled in the course rose .... from 1995 to 2005. (*steady*)
8 .... , I feel that we spend far too much money on space exploration. (*personal*)

4 Circle the correct words in the following extract.

> **"It takes more than good qualifications to become a good teacher." To what extent do you agree?**
>
> I had a mixture of teachers when I (1) *learned / studied* at school. Some were interesting and some were boring, some were (2) *excellence / excellent* and others were not so good. But what does it take to make a good teacher?
>
> One of the best teachers I have ever had was when I (3) *enrolled / took* a course in ancient history at university. I had never been very (4) *interest / interested* in history before, but this teacher managed to make the classes so (5) *entertainment / entertaining* that it was never dull. However, there is more to being a good teacher than personality. My history teacher at school had only a limited knowledge of his subject and I don't think that we (6) *knew / learned* a great deal from him. It is (7) *clear / clearly* that good qualifications can also be important.
>
> A good teacher needs to use their (8) *imagine / imagination* to create lessons that are (9) *helping / helpful* as well as (10) *education / educational*. They also need to gain the (11) *respect / respectful* of their students. Such teachers are usually (12) *extreme / extremely* popular with students. It is (13) *important / importantly* for teachers to be (14) *genuine / genuinely* interested in their students and their job in order to do it well. Perhaps there would be fewer problem students in schools if there were more 'good' teachers.

Verb confusion 2 - describing charts and figures

1 Tick the correct sentence in each pair.

1 a In 2002 the figure increased from 30% to 25%.

   b In 2002 the figure decreased from 30% to 25%.

2 a The flow chart displays the quantity of electricity consumed each year.

   b The flow chart shows the quantity of electricity consumed each year.

Describing charts

Graphs and charts can *show* facts:

*The two graphs **show** the number of people employed by the company in 1980 and 1990.*

We use *indicate* when we want to draw a conclusion about the figures in the charts:

*These figures **indicate** that the company is growing in size each year.*

We use *illustrate* to refer to evidence or proof of something:

*These figures **illustrate** the need for better management of our resources.*

We do not use *demonstrate*, *display* or *tell* to describe a chart. Compare the following:

*The salesman **demonstrated** the machine for us.* (= show how something works)

*Look at the figures **displayed** on the screen.* (= show on a screen)

*The girls' work was **displayed** for all to see.* (= make sure it can be easily seen)

*Did I **tell** you about my accident?* (= give a verbal or written account of a story)

Describing figures

If figures go up, we use *increase* or *rise*: *Temperatures **rose** in May.*

If the figures go down, we use *decrease* or *fall*: *The number of bats **fell** in 2004.*

If the figures stay the same, we use *remain steady* or *show little/no change*: *The figures **show little change** since 2001.*

2 Correct the mistake below.

I'm using slides to display the size of the problem.

I'm using slides to ....

3 Choose the correct verb to complete the sentences below.

1 The figures *illustrate* / *indicate* that enormous changes have occurred.

2 The book *demonstrates* / *tells* the story of a young boy and his life in Africa.

3 The greatest *increase* / *decrease* was in 1997, when it peaked at 56 tonnes.

4 The pie chart on the right *illustrates* / *tells* how serious this problem has become.

5 Most shops use shelves to *display* / *show* their products.

6 The figures reached a low in 2002, when they *fell* / *rose* to only 15%.

7 The two graphs *indicate* / *show* the total number of men and women enrolled.

8 If you are unsure how the camera works, I can *demonstrate* / *show* it to you.

Verb confusion 3 – money and problems

1 Tick the correct sentence in each pair.

1 a We are buying more and more money on cars each year.

  b We are spending more and more money on cars each year.

2 a We need to stop this problem as soon as possible.

  b We need to solve this problem as soon as possible.

Money: *buy* or *spend*?

We use *buy* to say what we bought or where we bought it: *'I **bought** a new jumper last week.' 'Where did you **buy** it?'* (= which shop did you buy it from)

We use *spend* to talk about money: *I **spent** over $250 on mobile phone calls last month.*

When we use *spend* by itself, the idea of money is understood in the sentence:

*We are **spending** more on petrol than ever before.* (= we are spending more money on petrol)

*We are **buying** more petrol than ever before.* (= the focus is on the petrol)

Problems: *avoid, fix, prevent, repair, resolve, solve*

We *fix* or *repair* something that is broken: *I took my watch to the jewellers to get it **fixed**.*

We *solve* problems: *We must try to **solve** the unemployment problem.*

We *resolve* difficult situations and issues: *What can we do to **resolve** this situation?*

We *prevent* problems so they do not happen (*prevent from* + *-ing; prevent* + noun / *-ing*):

*We need to do all we can to **prevent** this **from happening**.* (= to stop this happening)

2 Correct the mistake below.

It took me two hours to resolve the oil leak in my car.

It took me two hours ....

3 Fill in the blanks with a suitable verb from this unit.

1 It is important to teach children how to save money as well as how to .... it.

2 We must take the necessary action to .... this issue as quickly as possible.

3 If we are to use nuclear power, we have to do everything we can to .... a disaster like Chernobyl.

4 Winning a great deal of money cannot .... all of your problems.

5 How much did you .... on video games last year?

6 We closed all the windows to .... the rain from coming in.

7 I have to save a lot of money because I want to .... a car next year.

8 I can do most things at home but I can't .... electrical goods if they don't work.

Noun confusion 1 – money and work

1 Tick the correct sentence in each pair.

1 a Those who do manual work often earn less money.
   b Those who do manual work often earn less wages.
2 a People without computer skills find it difficult to get a job nowadays.
   b People without computer knowledge find it difficult to get a job nowadays.

- A *salary* is the total amount that a professional person is paid each year: *The marketing job offers opportunities to travel and an attractive salary.*
- A *wage* is the amount of money earned each week/month for casual or manual work: *Tim got a painting job with a wage of $400 per week.*
- We use *money* in a more general sense: *Nowadays people need to earn a lot more money to be able to buy a house.* (not ~~earn a lot more wages~~)

- *Job* refers to the type of work you do: *My job is to manage the staff.* or a particular task: *At home, my job is to do the ironing.*
- *Work* can be a noun or a verb and is used in a general sense: (uncountable noun) *It took a lot of work but I finished the project.* (verb) *My dad works in a bank.* *Workplace* is the place where you work: *It is better to train in the workplace rather than at a college.*
- *Knowledge* refers to facts you have studied over time, and *skills* refer to practical ability. Compare: *His knowledge of history is amazing. I have good typing skills.*
- We use *employment* and *unemployment* to talk about general work trends: *Unemployment figures fell this week. Employee = a worker, employer = a boss.*

2 Correct the mistake below.

Conditions at the factory were so bad that the employers decided to go on strike.

Conditions at the factory ....

3 Fill in the blanks with a suitable noun from this unit.

1 I paid more tax last week because of the extra .... I earned.
2 I know a lot about cars but I don't have the mechanical .... to fix them.
3 I read a book on the life and .... of Louis Pasteur, the famous scientist.
4 Joe's .... gave him a promotion and a higher ....
5 The problem of .... is a key issue for this year's election.
6 Moving house is such a big .... that I don't ever want to do it again.
7 Many workers can become ill if the conditions in their .... are not good.
8 I gave up my part-time .... as it was affecting my school ....

Test 9

1 Complete the sentences below with the correct form of one of the verbs in the box.

demonstrate	display (×2)	illustrate	show	tell

1 The televisions were .... at the front of the store.
2 The shop assistant .... the new televisions for us.
3 Martin used an image of a television to .... his point.
4 The departure times were .... on the television in our hotel room.
5 Jill .... us all about the new television she had just bought.
6 This chart .... the number of televisions sold in the last month.

2 Fill in the blanks in the following text. Use a different verb or phrase for each space.

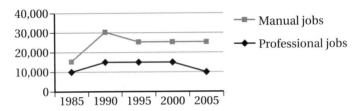

The graph (1) .... the number of professional and manual jobs available over a 20-year period. The number of manual job vacancies (2) .... dramatically between 1985 and 1990, but then it (3) .... over the next 5 years from 1990 to 1995. The number of professional jobs available also (4) .... between 1985 and 1990, reaching a peak of approximately 15,000. The figures then (5) .... until 2005, when they (6) .... to 10,000. The figures for manual jobs (7) .... since 1995. These figures (8) .... that, overall, there are fewer professional jobs available than manual jobs.

3 Choose the correct word to complete the following sentences.

1 The government is doing all it can to resolve this *problem / situation.*
2 Unemployment is one *issue / problem* that I don't think we will ever be able to solve.
3 Let's look at some ways to *prevent / solve* this situation from happening again.
4 By the end of the meeting, we had resolved all of the *issues / problems* raised by the staff.
5 We need to employ a Human Resources manager who can *prevent / solve* our staffing problems.
6 We finally *resolved / solved* the issue of who would wash up by buying a dishwasher.

4 Correct the 10 vocabulary mistakes in the following extract.

> *If we want to reduce unemployment, we need to pay workers more money for manual jobs. This will encourage people to work. To what extent do you agree or disagree?*
>
> In some countries, employed people are given money by the government to help them until they can find a suitable job. However, manual workers often receive salaries that are too low to live on; this means that there is little incentive for these people to work. One way to prevent the problem of unemployment would be for employees to pay their employers more money for jobs which do not require a great deal of knowledge, such as cleaning jobs.
>
> Paying more wages is only one way to encourage people to work, however. We also need to consider the working place. We need to ensure that it is safe and comfortable at all times, so that people can feel happy about going to work.
>
> If we want to resolve unemployment from increasing, then we need to do what we can to encourage people to continue working. This situation will not be solved unless we deal with the issue of working conditions as well as money.

5 Complete the following conversation with the correct form of either *spend* or *buy*.

Teacher: What kinds of things do young people generally spend their money on?

Student: That's difficult to say because girls tend to (1) .... different things from boys. Many of the young girls I know prefer to (2) .... their money on clothes, for example. They also like (3) .... lots of accessories like jewellery or make-up. But my brother, for example, (4) .... most of his money on video games. He (5) .... at least one new one per month; I'd say he (6) .... about $100 a month on video games.

Teacher: Can you tell me about something you have bought recently?

Student: Erm, I (7) .... a new mobile phone last month. It cost me quite a lot, and then I (8) .... over $200 on phone calls, so it's been a really expensive purchase so far!

Noun confusion 2 – advertising, travel and young people

1 Tick the correct sentence in each pair.

1 a Advertising on TV is the best way of increasing your business.

   b Advertisement on TV is the best way of increasing your business.

2 a How was your travel to Canada?

   b How was your trip to Canada?

- *Advertise* is the verb and *advertisement* (it can be shortened to *advert*) is the noun. We can also use *commercial* to refer to TV advertisements: *I saw a really funny* ***advertisement / commercial*** *on TV last night.* We use *advertising* to refer to the industry: *My sister works in **advertising**.*

- We use *journey* or *trip* to talk about getting from A to B: *The **journey / trip** to Australia was really long.*

- *Travel* is a verb and an uncountable noun which refers to taking journeys in general: *We **travelled** for hours before we saw any sign of life. Air **travel** is very cheap these days.*

- *Trip* can also refer to a holiday or an excursion: *I needed a break so I decided to take a **trip** to the coast.* (not ~~I decided to take a travel~~)

- We usually use *youth* to refer to a stage of life: *I did a lot of travelling in my **youth**.* It is rarely used to talk about people; instead, we use *young person* or *young people*.

2 Correct the mistake below.

I wish I had something to read on the travel.

I wish I had something ....

3 Fill in the blanks with a suitable word or phrase from this unit.

1 Have you packed any snacks for the train ....?

2 The .... we placed in train stations bring us the most business.

3 We need to give the .... in our society a lot more opportunities if we want them to grow into responsible adults.

4 I'll apply for a job in .... when I finish my marketing course.

5 I was very unhappy with the skiing .... organised by your company.

6 Would you prefer to .... by train or by plane?

7 Is it more effective to .... a product on TV or in magazines?

8 We are looking for a .... with an interest in computers to fill the post.

When do I need to use an apostrophe?

1 Tick the correct sentence in each pair.

1 a I am sorry but I wont be able to come to your party on Saturday.
  b I am sorry but I won't be able to come to your party on Saturday.
2 a Children's toys are much more sophisticated now than in the past.
  b Childrens toys are much more sophisticated now than in the past.

We use apostrophes
- to shorten words and show that some letters have been left out:
  cannot → can't; could not → couldn't; do not → don't; he will → he'll;
  will not → won't; she would → she'd.
  These contractions are mostly used in spoken or informal language:
  *I **can't** find Peter anywhere – he isn't in the staffroom or in his office.*
- after people or animals to show possession: *Mary's hat, the cat's food dish*

We do not use an apostrophe
- with possessive pronouns, such as *its, ours, theirs, yours*:
  *The caterpillar stays in **its** cocoon until metamorphosis is complete.* (not ~~it's cocoon~~)
- when we add *s* to a singular noun to make it plural, even if we are using a
  commonly abbreviated word: *CDs, TVs* (not: ~~CD's, TV's~~)
- to show possession with things. Instead, we use *of the*: *the leg **of the** chair* (not ~~the chair's leg~~)

2 Correct the mistake below.

The male Emperor penguin looks after it's young.

The male Emperor ....

3 Correct the mistakes in the sentences below. Some sentences may have more than one mistake, some may be correct.

1 I put Jack coat on a hanger in the cupboard.
2 I cant understand why older people dont like modern music.
3 I bought three new CD's this week.
4 The dog wagged it's tail when it saw the children.
5 Fresh avocado's on sale today!
6 Which one is mine and which one is her's?
7 Can you put this in the car's boot for me?
8 It's about time you fixed that car of yours.

30 Common spelling errors

1 Tick the correct sentence in each pair.

1 a *Some people believe that there should be more women in goverment.*
   b *Some people believe that there should be more women in government.*
2 a *It is the responsibility of every contry to protect the environment.*
   b *It is the responsibility of every country to protect the environment.*

Some words are spelled incorrectly because they are similar to another word:

- *to* or *too*? *I want to go **to** the park. I wanted a new computer but ended up with a printer **too**.* (= as well)
- *there* or *their*? *Your book is **there**, on the table. Students must buy **their** books before the start of term.*
- *though* or *through*? *Several students chose Russian **though** they had never studied a language before. The tour guide led the group **through** some areas of ancient rainforest.*

Sometimes there is confusion over British and American spellings:
e.g. *programme* = British   *program* = American
☆ Use either British or American spellings, but do not mix the two different styles:
(UK) *It's my **favourite colour**.* or: (US) *It's my **favorite color**.* (not ~~It's my favourite color.~~)

The following words are also often spelled incorrectly. Pay particular attention to those with double letters: *accommodation, advertisement, always, benefit, beginning, business, commercial, country, different, environment, government, nowadays, occurred, passenger, restaurant, teacher, which*

2 Correct the mistakes below.

It says, 'Two star acomodation available. Includes breakfast. Good resturant.'

It says, 'Two star ....'

3 Correct the spelling mistakes in the sentences below.

1 The goverment of my contry has introduced a new system to encourage recycling.
2 I am not sure wich of the students has brought there camera.
3 Nowdays you need to be sure to read advertisments carefully.
4 It makes good comercial sense to invest time and money in your busines.
5 My geography teatcher taught us a lot about the enviroment.
6 The passangers had to walk throught several corridors to reach the plane.
7 My sister has to watch her favourite TV programme every nite.
8 There are many benifits in using the internet to book acomodation.

52

Test 10

1 Write the underlined words without a contraction.

1 My dog <u>won't</u> eat tinned food. ....
2 <u>He'd</u> never seen a kangaroo before. ....
3 <u>We'd</u> like to see the menu, please. ....
4 <u>She's</u> already got a car. ....
5 We <u>couldn't</u> see any fish in the river. ....
6 <u>They've</u> been waiting for ages. ....
7 <u>They're</u> leaving in the morning. ....
8 <u>It's</u> a shame you <u>can't</u> stay. ....

2 Add 8 apostrophes to the following conversation.

Sally: Im going to need some help to clean up tomorrow. Are you busy?

Tim: Ill be able to do a bit early on but then Ive got to go to the airport. Mums plane lands at 12:00.

Sally: Oh, yes. Id forgotten your mum was coming. How long is she here for?

Tim: Shes only here for a few weeks.

Sally: Oh, so she wont be here for your party, then?

Tim: No. That reminds me, I havent got any petrol in my car. Can I borrow yours?

3 Complete the following text with a suitable form of *journey, travel* or *trip*.

> Describe a holiday you remember well. You should say
>
> where you went
> how you travelled
> what you did there
> and say why you remember it so well

One holiday I remember was a bike-riding (1) .... I took to France when I was 19. I went with a friend. First we (2) .... to London by train and then we had another train (3) .... to get to Dover, where we caught the ferry. It was a really rough crossing and my friend was sick the whole (4) .... We had planned to spend two or three weeks (5) .... around France on our bikes and camping, but it rained constantly and after only a few days, our tents were soaking wet and we decided to go home. On the (6) .... home we felt quite disappointed, but I'll never forget that (7) .... because it was my first holiday abroad without my parents.

4 Correct the 12 vocabulary and spelling mistakes in the following text.

'There is far too much advertising on TV these days.' Do you agree?

Nowdays, if you watch a programme on a commercial TV station, you should expect to watch a large number of advertising to. It seems that television advertise is the price we pay for free-to-air TV. But is this price higher than we realise? Not only are constant advertisings annoying, but they also mean that youths are being constantly told to buy things they dont need or eat things that aren't healthy. It often seems as through children are being specifically targeted by the commercial industry because they make there commercials very colorful and loud, and so even very young children are attracted to them. I think it is important to realise that TV's are a very effective teaching tool and we should therefore take more care with how this medium is used.

5 Complete the crossword below.

Across →
3 advantage
4 the person who leads a class
5 our surroundings
9 currently
11 a person who travels on a bus, plane or train
12 a place to eat
13 I'm not sure .... one to choose.
14 England is a ....
15 not the same

Down ↓
1 the start
2 a place to stay
6 the opposite of *never*
7 happened
8 another word for *commerce*
10 we use this to sell a product

54

Answer key

Unit 1
1 1 a
   2 b
2 not the same as mine
3 1 the internet
   2 rivers
   3 America
   4 the number
   5 the same
   6 the USA
   7 the greatest
   8 The moon, the earth

Unit 2
1 1 b
   2 a
2 women studying science increased
3 1 children
   2 men
   3 people
   4 it
   5 was
   6 classes
   7 person
   8 watches

Unit 3
1 1 b
   2 b
2 amount of garbage
3 1 ...very good **piece of** advice about...
   2 ...the **amount of time** it took us...
   3 ...great deal of **knowledge** to...
   4 The **information** we were
     given...**was** not very helpful.
   5 ...to see so **much garbage** left there.
   6 ...there **was** so **much** traffic...
   7 ...and do **some** shopping.
   8 The **furniture**...**was** quite old but **it was** very comfortable.

Test 1
1 1 is
   2 is
   3 is
   4 ideas

5 advice, was
6 students
7 similarities
8 are

2 1 The table
   2 The number one
   3 the largest
   4 The United Kingdom
   5 the list
   6 the United States
   7 the Faroe Islands
   8 the world
   9 Sweden
   10 Malta
   11 the same
   12 the internet
3 1 Is
   2 Is there
   3 Is there
   4 How much
   5 Are there
   6 How much
   7 How many
   8 Is there
4 1 piece of advice
   2 houses
   3 companies
   4 people
   5 children
   6 plastic
   7 transport
   8 birds
5 (1) **Globalisation** has had; on many (2) **parts** of the world; some of (3) **the** most remote; of (4) **the** world; connect to (5) **the** internet; However, (6) **there are** (7) **advantages** and (8) **disadvantages** to this; One (9) **disadvantage**, for example; local businesses (10) **have** to reduce; stop young (11) **people** moving; more remote (12) **areas**; a young person (13) **has** the chance; news from around the world (14) **is** available.

Unit 4

1 1 b

  2 b

2 watches TV for 8 hours every day

3 1 ...according to what they **believe**.

  2 ...government **spends** too much...

  3 ...in my country **send** their...

  4 ...people **travel** to very distant...

  5 I **hope** it is not...

  6 The female hen **lays** on average...

  7 Younger drivers **are** more likely...

  8 ...doctors **agree** that the only...

Unit 5

1 1 b

  2 a

2 Thousands of people

3 1 thousands

  2 three hundred

  3 three and a half billion

  4 six hundred dollars

  5 three quarters of a million

  6 Millions of

  7 six hundred

  8 one and a half billion

Unit 6

1 1 b

  2 b

2 there were a lot more little shops

3 1 ...countries **there are** many...

  2 **There is** no clear trend...

  3 ...and **there are** no factories...

  4 Fortunately, **there are** still a lot...

  5 ...so **there aren't** any large...

  6 ...chart, **there is** a large gap...

  7 In 1990 **there were** 3 million...

  8 How much work **is there** to do?

Test 2

1 1 gets up

  2 starts

  3 is

  4 has

  5 leaves

  6 wakes

  7 gets up

  8 prefers

  9 catches

  10 makes

  11 get dressed

  12 leave

2 1 g

  2 f

  3 h

  4 b

  5 i

3 agriculture (1) **is** very important; our farmers (2) **grow** a wide; this (3) **helps** to reduce; which also (4) **reduces** the price; their day (5) **begins** very; often (6) **work** until late; weather also (7) **makes** their working; many farmers (8) **feel** that; We (9) **need** to encourage; chains (10) **take** a large; The government (11) **need/needs** to address; that they (12) **protect** this.

4 2 two million

  3 one and three quarter million

  4 one and a half million

  5 a million *or* one million

  6 a million *or* one million

  7 nine hundred thousand

  8 three quarters of a million

5 1 There

  2 They

  3 there

  4 They

  5 It

  6 There

  7 they

  8 there

Unit 7

1 1 b

  2 a

2 someone who/that can play the piano

3 1 ...problems **that** can occur...

  2 ...teacher **who/that** inspired...

  3 ...teenagers **who/that** do not feel...

  4 ...those **who/that** do not have...

  5 People **who/that** work with...

  6 People **who/that** continue...

  7 I understand **what** you mean.

  8 The chart **that** is on the left...

Unit 8

1 1 b
    2 b

2 but James hates it

3 1 or
    2 and
    3 or
    4 but
    5 or
    6 or not
    7 but
    8 or

Unit 9

1 1 b
    2 b

2 We are going to play tennis. Do you want to join us?

3 1 does
    2 are
    3 –
    4 have
    5 do
    6 is
    7 have
    8 –

Test 3

1 1 ...or even a television at home.
    2 ...and we walked along the beach collecting shells.
    3 ...but I got a little lost near the end.
    4 ...or not to go to the party.
    5 ...but not entry to the museum.
    6 ...or a laptop at home.
    7 ...but I don't like coffee.
    8 ...and dinner.

2 C: ...plenty to do, (1) **but** I (2) **do** not want... (3) **Can you** suggest...
    TA: ...island (4) **that** is only...
    TA: ...there (5) **aren't** any flights...
    C: How much (6) **does** it cost...
    C: (7) **Does** that include the ferry?
    TA: ...all transport (8) **and** hotel...

3 1 The students **that/who** struggle...
    2 ...grandmother **that/who** first...
    3 ...sure **what** we have to write...
    4 ...an instrument **that** is used to...
    5 ...apologise for **what** I said...
    6 Venus is a planet **that** you can...
    7 ...creatures **that** live in rivers...
    8 The people **that/who** I know...
    ☆ Numbers 6 and 8 do not need a relative pronoun.

4 1 did
    2 are
    3 have, have
    4 is
    5 is
    6 Do, am
    7 does
    8 have

5 1 or
    2 and
    3 but
    4 and
    5 or
    6 what
    7 but
    8 but
    9 that
    10 or
    11 don't
    12 and

Unit 10

1 1 b
    2 a

2 can't smoke in this restaurant

3 1 ...you **can find** internet facilities...
    2 We **should not** accept this...
    3 ...we must **try** our best...
    4 We **don't have** to stop...
    5 **Can we solve** the problem...?
    6 **Do you need** to take any food...
    7 ...you really **must study** harder...
    8 ...we **have to leave** our mobile...

Unit 11

1 1 a
   2 b
2 over $300 buying food for the party
3 1 to buy
   2 to ice skate
   3 doing
   4 stirring
   5 to help
   6 choosing
   7 to study
   8 having

Unit 12

1 1 b
   2 a
2 in spite of being the youngest player
3 1 to understand
   2 to cook
   3 presenting
   4 getting
   5 causing
   6 to see
   7 receiving
   8 staying

Test 4

1 1 Can you buy *or* Can I buy
   2 Yes, you can. You don't have to go
   3 Do we have to hand
   4 No, we don't have to give
   5 Does Joe need to take
   6 he shouldn't go
2 1 They went to the cinema instead of going to school.
   2 I enjoyed the party despite not knowing anyone there.
   3 I am optimistic about the future in spite of there being so many problems in the world.
   4 We all enjoyed the course despite having to work so hard.
   5 My parents gave me some money instead of buying me a present.
   6 The company went out of business in spite of spending thousands of dollars on marketing.

3 I really (1) **enjoy listening** to music; everyone (2) **should look** after their body and (3) **try to** keep fit; soccer team, but I (4) **had to** turn it down because my parents (5) **wouldn't allow** me (6) **to** take it; my parents (7) **suggested studying** a musical instrument; If you (8) **want to** be a good musician, you really (9) **must work** hard and (10) **keep practising** every day; (11) **spending a lot of time studying** so I couldn't do it then; I'm (12) **looking forward to learning** to play.
4 1 to show
   2 to study
   3 to waste
   4 to speak
   5 practising
   6 speaking
   7 making
   8 speaking
   9 to get
5 1 happy to do
   2 impossible to mark, too difficult to understand.
   3 excited getting
   4 too expensive to buy
   5 not fit enough to win
   6 sad watching

Unit 13

1 1 b
   2 b
2 not allowed to skateboard in the park
3 1 I suggest you **go** and **do** your...
   2 ...made me ~~to~~ clean up my room...
   3 ...allowed **to use** mobile phones...
   4 ...forbidden **to smoke** in many...
   5 ...I finally made ~~work~~ my new DVD player **work**.
   6 ...not **to leave** their windows...
   7 ...permit **you to** enter the museum...
   8 ...suggested **going/(that)we go** to the park...

Unit 14

1 1 a
   2 b
2 I had to stop to tie my shoelace

3 1 working
    2 to buy
    3 to open
    4 to send
    5 to have
    6 visiting
    7 adding
    8 walking

Unit 15
1 1 a
    2 b
2 very pleased about their final results
3 1 good at *or* interested in
    2 difference between
    3 advantage of
    4 increase in *or* rise in
    5 interested in
    6 percentage of *or* number of
    7 example of
    8 decrease in *or* drop in *or* fall in

Test 5
1 1 to borrow
    2 to bring
    3 to store
    4 reserving/you to reserve
    5 to copy
    6 emailing/you to email
    7 to use
    8 completing/(that) you complete
2 the number (1) **of** people; difference
    (2) **between** the two sets; the
    percentage (3) **of** people living; a rise
    (4) **in** population figures; The biggest
    increase (5) **in** population; decrease (6)
    in the number (7) **of** people living; the
    number (8) **of** inhabitants
3 1 at
    2 give up
    3 working
    4 at
    5 coming
    6 to answer
    7 with
    8 to brush

4 1 to stop people smoking
    2 many areas of our life
    3 One important example of this
    4 the disadvantages of smoking
    5 be worried about this problem
    6 advise people not to smoke
    7 tried increasing
    8 tried to find
    9 allow smoking
    10 people are not permitted to smoke
    11 make people stop smoking
    12 the number of cigarettes
    13 I suggest (that) all governments
        adopt
    14 prevent more children taking up

Unit 16
1 1 b
    2 a
2 looking for my car keys
3 1 about
    2 to
    3 for
    4 about
    5 about *or* of
    6 at
    7 with
    8 for

Unit 17
1 1 b
    2 b
2 walk to work during the train strike
3 1 in
    2 at
    3 for
    4 on
    5 to, in
    6 at
    7 in
    8 at

Unit 18
1 1 a
    2 b
2 in front of the post office

3 1 ...a good quality **of** life.
   2 ...a long period **of** time...
   3 ...as a result **of** my illness.
   4 The government **of** my country...
   5 I wrote a letter **of** complaint...
   6 ...number **of** different types **of** cars...
   7 The leader **of** the opposition...the result **of** the election.
   8 ...instead **of going** to a restaurant... what type **of** food we wanted.

Test 6
1 1 think about
   2 agree with
   3 teach you about
   4 know about
   5 find out about
   6 looking for
   7 looking at
2 1 I agree **with** what you are saying...
   2 The difference **between** your...
   3 ...the importance **of** checking...
   4 Fruit bats emerge **at** night to feed...
   5 ...tomorrow morning **at** 10:00?
   6 ...this coffee shop **for** six months.
   7 My birthday is **on** 8th November...
   8 ...piano lessons **in** July last year.
3 1 at
   2 in
   3 for
   4 at
   5 on
   6 at
   7 on
   8 in
   9 at
  10 for
4 1 with
   2 for
   3 for
   4 to
   5 because
   6 at
   7 because of
   8 to

5 1 the hotel not being finished
   2 the water being so dirty
   3 swimming
   4 the weather being so bad
   5 it being covered by cloud
   6 the bus breaking down
   7 eating undercooked chicken

Unit 19
1 1 a
   2 b
2 was given this painting by my grandmother
3 1 The house was **sold** for over...
   2 The class **was** allowed to eat...
   3 The potatoes **are carried** along...they **are washed** and **peeled**.
   4 The teacher **was** told to take...
   5 Smoking **is not allowed** in any...
   6 ...was being **renovated** when...
   7 Bus tickets can **be bought** at...
   8 New employees **are** instructed...

Unit 20
1 1 b
   2 b
2 should be worn at all times
3 1 is checked for quality.
   2 under 16 are not permitted to work.
   3 are being washed at the moment.
   4 will be repaired this afternoon.
   5 has been sold at last.
   6 was torn.
   7 are paid more for working at the weekend.
   8 are given off by burning tyres.

Unit 21
1 1 b
   2 b
2 cost over 200 million dollars to build
3 1 ...it is **acceptable** *or* **all right** to...
   2 **Children** today are much more...
   3 The **number** of people...in the **year 2001** was **3.5 million**.
   4 ...create a **great deal** *or* a **large number** of jobs...

5 A large amount of **money** is spent on developing tourism. (*N.B. not all capitals*)
6 ...than the **males**.
7 ...but the **percentage** that...
8 gains 90 **kilos** *or* **kilograms** per day

Test 7

1 2 the principal
   3 the government
   4 the burglar
   5 the hospital staff
   6 the nation
   2 Each year the principal chooses the most improved student.
   3 The government has/have passed a new law to make the dumping of waste illegal.
   4 I realised the burglar had stolen my keys during the break-in.
   5 The hospital staff are treating Simon for minor burns.
   6 The nation will elect our new government on June 20th.

2 Behavioural training should (1) **be done** on; This type of training (2) **is used** to; Obedience training should (3) **be done** often; his meal (4) **is associated** with a reward; puppies (5) **are injured** because; The house can (6) **be made** of any; It can (7) **be used** for house-training; If your puppy (8) **is rewarded** with; feet should (9) **be placed** firmly; the puppy (10) **is given** a treat.

3 1 is made
   2 is chosen
   3 is stripped
   4 is soaked
   5 is then heated
   6 not be allowed
   7 be placed
   8 are sewn
   9 is finished
   10 are used (by indigenous people)

4 The graph shows the (1) **number** of people; the types of (2) **things** *or* **products** that (3) **are bought**; most

money (4) **is spent** on travel; amount of money is (5) **spent** on groceries; are for the (6) **year** 1995; The (7) **percentage** of people; it took (8) **a long time** for people; people still (9) **want to** visit shops; 75% say they have (10) **received** good value for money.

Unit 22

1 1 b
   2 b
2 hard for his exams
3 1 well
   2 sharply
   3 gradual
   4 clear, easily
   5 strongly
   6 Severe
   7 Unfortunately
   8 vitally

Unit 23

1 1 b
   2 a
2 good pair of sports shoes
3 1 I can't tell the **difference** between...
   2 ...was **invaluable** in the exam.
   3 It is important to eat a **healthy** diet...
   4 ...no **female** members of parliament.
   5 I can't study in **silence**...
   6 ...who is loved is a **happy** child.
   7 Both **women and men** need to be included...
   8 ...we were making too much **noise**.

Unit 24

1 1 a
   2 a
2 to enrol in an English language course
3 1 learning
   2 enrol in
   3 know
   4 study
   5 learn
   6 studying
   7 know
   8 study

Test 8

1
1 confidence
2 development
3 healthy
4 responsibility
5 significance
6 difference
7 natural
8 beneficial

2 people are more (1) **concerned** these days about being (2) **successful** in their career; very well (3) **educated** if you want; life is also more (4) **competitive** these days; to study (5) **hard** at school; make a big (6) **difference** in getting the job; speak English (7) **well**, so it's (8) **important** to study languages.

3
1 significantly
2 slightly
3 sharply
4 incredibly
5 Sadly
6 extremely
7 steadily
8 Personally

4
1 studied
2 excellent
3 took
4 interested
5 entertaining
6 learned
7 clear
8 imagination
9 helpful
10 educational
11 respect
12 extremely
13 important
14 genuinely

Unit 25

1
1 b
2 b

2 illustrate the size of the problem

3
1 indicate
2 tells
3 increase
4 illustrates
5 display
6 fell
7 show
8 demonstrate

Unit 26

1
1 b
2 b

2 to fix *or* repair the oil leak in my car

3
1 spend
2 resolve
3 prevent
4 solve
5 spend
6 prevent
7 buy
8 fix – *or* – repair

Unit 27

1
1 a
2 a

2 were so bad that the employees decided to go on strike

3
1 money
2 skills
3 work
4 employer, salary
5 unemployment
6 job
7 workplace
8 job, work

Test 9

1
1 displayed
2 demonstrated
3 illustrate
4 displayed
5 told
6 shows

2
1 shows
2 rose *or* increased
3 fell *or* dropped
4 rose *or* increased
5 remained the same *or* showed no change
6 dropped *or* fell
7 have remained the same *or* have not changed
8 indicate

3
1 situation
2 problem
3 prevent
4 issues
5 solve
6 resolved

4 In some countries, (1) **unemployed** people; workers often receive (2) **wages** that are; One way to (3) **solve** the problem; would be for (4) **employers** to pay their (5) **employees** more money; a great deal of (6) **skill**, such as cleaning jobs; Paying more (7) **money** is only; consider the (8) **workplace**; want to (9) **prevent** unemployment; not be (10) **resolved** unless

5
1 buy
2 spend
3 buying
4 spends
5 buys
6 spends
7 bought
8 spent

Unit 28
1
1 a
2 b
2 to read on the trip *or* journey
3
1 trip *or* journey
2 advertisements
3 young people
4 advertising
5 trip
6 travel
7 advertise
8 young person

Unit 29
1
1 b
2 a
2 penguin looks after its young
3
1 I put **Jack's** coat...
2 I **can't** understand; people **don't** like modern music.
3 ...three new **CDs** this week.
4 ...wagged **its** tail...
5 Fresh **avocados** on sale today!
6 ...which one is **hers**?
7 ...in the **boot of the car** for me?
8 *correct*

Unit 30
1
1 b
2 b
2 accommodation available. Includes breakfast. Good restaurant.
3
1 government, country
2 which, their
3 Nowadays advertisements
4 commercial, business
5 teacher, environment
6 passengers, through
7 night
8 benefits, accommodation

Test 10
1
1 will not
2 He had
3 We would
4 She has
5 could not
6 They have
7 They are
8 It is, cannot
2 **I'm** going to need; **I'll** be able; then **I've** got to; **Mum's** plane; **I'd** forgotten; **She's** only; she **won't** be here; I **haven't** got any petrol
3
1 trip
2 travelled
3 trip *or* journey
4 trip *or* journey
5 travelling
6 journey *or* trip
7 trip

4 (1) **Nowadays**, if you watch; a large number of (2) **advertisements** – *or* – **commercials** (3) **too**; television (4) **advertising** is the price we pay; constant (5) **advertisements** *or* **commercials** annoying; mean that (6) **young people** are being; things they (7) **don't** need; seems as (8) **though** children; targeted by the (9) **advertising** industry; they make (10) **their** commercials very (11) **colourful** and loud; realise that (12) **TVs** are a very effective teaching tool

5 Across
3 benefit
4 teacher
5 environment
9 nowadays
11 passenger
12 restaurant
13 which
14 country
15 different
Down
1 beginning
2 accommodation
6 always
7 occurred
8 business
10 advertisement

Acknowledgements

For Fraser and Alex

The author would like to thank Julie Moore for her help at the start of this project and Thérèse Tobin for her invaluable advice and guidance.

Illustrated by Julian Mosedale

The Cambridge Learner Corpus
This book is based on information from the Cambridge Learner Corpus, a collection of over 90,000 exam papers from Cambridge ESOL. It shows real mistakes students make, and highlights which parts of English cause particular problems for learners.

The Cambridge Learner Corpus has been developed jointly with the University of Cambridge ESOL Examinations and forms part of the Cambridge International Corpus.

To find out more, visit
www.cambridge.org/elt/corpus